Timeless Wisdom: Quotations *from* East and West

Editor

Hazem I. Kira

This book is dedicated to my mom, a giving soul for whom I can never repay, and to Dr. A. K. Saeed for opening my eyes to the inherent wisdom embedded in all cultures and traditions.

Contents

Introduction

E Pluribus Unum
(From Many, One)

Never before have the open secrets of both East and the West been so close to one's fingertips. Huddled in the forthcoming pages are not token authors from the "other" side of the world, but a balanced collection of unearthed gems to be found in any one quote book. Ideas born from both halves of our diminutive planet by the world's greatest thinkers—warriors, philosophers, poets, academics, saints, and prophets alike—who reflect, with us in tow, on such subjects as the nature of time, love, morality, beauty, success, the divine, and for that matter the very words we utter. It is in this exhaustive labor of love that you will find inspiration, wisdom, and words ripe for the proverbial picking.

As a child of both East and West, I started this book many years ago on my journey of self-discovery. To my delight, I have discovered many of humanity's innermost secrets. Each quote, herein, is a piece of a jigsaw puzzle that when fitted together forms a picture of humanity's most sublime reflections and triumphs.

Born in the East are the written word, the foundations of science and math, alongside Confucius, Mandela, Tolstoy, Gandhi, Jesus, Moses, and Muhammad. Celebrated in the West are the Magna Carta, modern notions of individualism and democracy, and the expansion of scientific knowledge that allows humans to shape their environment in extraordinary ways.

Unfortunately, the open secrets—those that sit in front of us and beg to be laid bare—are often overlooked with our unease or partial exposure of the "other." Overlooked is the elegant truth that nations, much like individuals, have insights forged from centuries of history, struggle, and debate. In the end, knowledge is not a one way street or even a two way street, says A. K. Saeed, rather "it evolves multidirectionally."

Bon Appétit,
Hazem I. Kira

About This Book

One never knows from which spring knowledge will flow. Recently, while in the final phase of this collection, I sat down with my six-year-old niece—my little bundle of joy—on a camping trip and read to her some of the wisdom found from both sides of our "global coin."

After catching a glimpse of the "Eastern" and "Western" designations, she asked, "Why use only those two, how about Northern and Southern?" At first I laughed. But then I found myself prompted to revisit those designations, as well as the concept of identity formation.

References of Eastern and Western people are seen in over three millennia of literature, history, and culture. The commonly used terms "orient"—from the Latin *oriri*, "to rise" from the east—and "occident"—from the Latin *occidere*, "falls down" (in reference to the sun setting in the west)—have shifted, over the years, from a neutral geographic description to generic assumptions of the "other." Today, Northern/Southern delineations are increasingly more common, but often are in reference to distinctions between First—and Third-World nations.

A major problem that I encountered in preparing this book is that not everyone falls neatly into one category. I myself was born in the northeastern tip of Africa, on the steps of the pyramids of Giza, deep in the concrete jungles of Cairo. On my fifth birthday, my family and I moved to the United States. My father, who was then in the diplomatic core, came to serve out his full tour at the Egyptian Consulate in San Francisco. Having been born in the East and raised in the West, what then is my designation? Am I not a hybrid of the two?

But then came even trickier labels, including those that I was tempted to redefine altogether. For instance, which category do the Greeks fall into? The Greek Church, even today, is known as the "Eastern Orthodox Church," and the notable Greek figure, Aristotle, lived much of his life in what is now part of modern-day Turkey. Since the fall of the Roman Empire in 476 by Odoacer, a Germanic general, the world has largely been divided into the Greek East and the Latin West. In the end, I decided to stay within the lines drawn out by most modern-day Western preferences. Aristotle, thus, will stay a modern Western construct.

That said, it is important to reflect upon Benedict Anderson's assertion that nations are actually "imagined political communities" which dwell in a constant state of defining and redefining their languages, borders, and cultures. In truth, borders—demarcations of any kind—are claims found, not in nature, but in the *collective imagination* of a people. Thus, how we see ourselves today, is not how we imagined ourselves a few years ago or even in a few years, henceforth.

The final challenge I faced in preparing this collection was in determining the categories. This was a particularly difficult task because a question mulled over by a South African in the twentieth century is not the same question asked by a French peasant in the fifteenth century. Arnold Tonynbee, the great historian, tells us that history must be seen through the lens of challenge and response, as opposed to cause and effect. In other words, events are not deterministic or automatic, but rather every situation has *unique challenges* and thus requires *unique responses*. It is also the reason why similar questions (e.g., what is considered beautiful) may lead to varied conclusions. For example, the great teacher and activist, Helen Keller, who was both blind and deaf, argues that the "best and most beautiful things in the world cannot be seen or even touched," rather "they must be felt with the heart."

How then to categorize these broad subjects? The answer came when I considered S. I. Hyakawa's "ladder of abstraction." On his "ladder," one can climb to higher and higher levels of abstraction (in language) or lower and lower into more specifics. Politicians, for example, tend to use generic abstract terms to speak to a broad demographic, whereas academics prefer more specific terms. As such, for the purpose of this book, I decided to climb to the higher levels of the ladder and use generic subject headings such as "beauty" and "ambition." Finally, throughout the book, I tried to maintain a balanced weight of quotes from each side of our "global coin." This was not always easy, since most works are not easily found or translated into English.

This collection will no doubt lead each person to their own conclusions. As for this author, it has cemented one overarching fact, that we, as humans, can learn from each other, and that when we choose to self-censor the words we listen to or the ideas we ponder—simply because they may come from another tribe or ethnicity—we succeed only in limiting our awareness of reality, creating false choices, and dooming ourselves to inevitable folly.

Finally, the fact that a quote is cited should not indicate agreement or disagreement. Additionally, I wholly concede that I am far from being an example of even the most true and virtuous quotes found herein. To improve future editions, suggestions from readers are most welcome. These could be new quotations or corrections in this first edition. Please submit such contributions to Kira@TimelessWisdom.info.

We should never be ashamed to approve truth and acquire it no matter what its source might be.

—*Al-Kindi*

We hold these Truths to be self-evident...

—*U.S. Declaration of Independence*

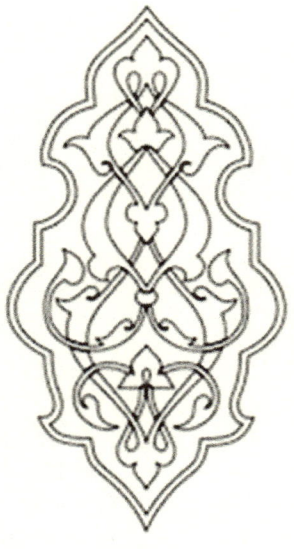

Ability

Ability | Eastern

Smooth seas do not make able sailors.

—African proverb

The well-being of the soul can only be obtained after that of the body has been secured.

—Moses Maimonides

The fact that the poor are alive is clear proof of their ability.

—Muhammad Yunus

Give sail to ability.

—Japanese proverb

The difference between what we do and what we are capable of doing would suffice to solve most of the world's problems.

—Mahatma Gandhi

If we pay no attention to each man's intellectual endowments and capacities and push down those who rise to a high position in order to make all equal, the world will not progress.

—Sun Yat-sen

It had come out of the cover of its nest and stood face to face with the boundless sky but it was not yet aware of its powers. [Suddenly] it realized in its bones that it was a flying creature. A breath of life fanned through the lifeless frame. The drooping wings began to quiver for a take-off. In the twinkling of an eye the urge to fl y shook its whole frame and it jumped off as it had received a shock. The next moment the bird of courage was traversing space like an eagle.

—Abul Kalam Azad

Ability | Western

Give me the place to stand, and I shall move the earth.

—Archimedes

Hide not your talents... What's a sundial in the shade?

—Benjamin Franklin

Natural ability without education has more often raised a man to glory and virtue than education without natural ability.

—Marcus T. Cicero

We judge ourselves by what we feel capable of doing, while others judge us by what we have already done.

—Henry W. Longfellow

In the country of the blind, the one-eyed man is king.

—Erasmus

The less their ability, the more their conceit.

—Ahad HaAm (Asher Zvi Hirsch Ginsberg)

The test of a first-rate intelligence is the ability to hold two opposed ideas in the mind at the same time.

—F. Scott Fitzgerald

Every man believes that he has a greater possibility.

—Ralph Waldo Emerson

Terry Malloy: I could have been a contender.

—Budd Schulberg

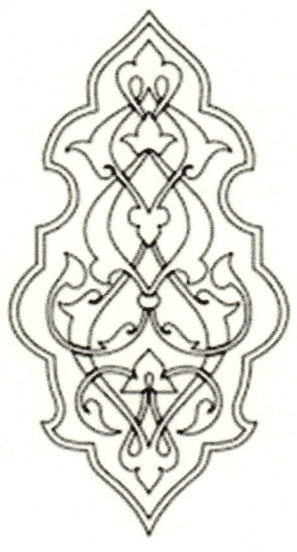

Action

Action | Eastern

Chih-nan hsing-i
Knowledge is difficult; Action is easy.

—Sun Yat-sen

Faith alone is not enough, unless works too are joined to it.
—St. Augustine of Hippo

The superior man acts before he speaks.

—Confucius (K'ung-Fu-Tzu)

To sew patch upon patch and be patient is better than writing petitions to great men for clothing.

—Sa'di

There is no easy walk to freedom.

—Nelson Mandela

When you are working for others, let it be with the same zeal as if it were for yourself.

—Confucius

Let piety and faithfulness mark every action.

—Abu Hanifah

Vision without action is a daydream. Action without vision is a nightmare.
—Japanese proverb

A bird in hand is better than ten on a tree.

—Egyptian proverb

Actions are judged by intention.
—Muhammad (Muhammad ibn Abdullah)
Sahih al-Bukhari (prophetic traditions)

The world is three days: As for yesterday, it has vanished, along with all that was in it. As for tomorrow, you may never see it. As for today, it is yours, so work in it.

—Hassan al-Basri

Action | Western

This is no time for romantic illusions and empty philosophical debates about freedom. This is a time for action.

—Martin Luther King Jr.
Address to the Southern Christian Leadership Conference, 1967

We tire the night in thought, the day in toil.

—Francis Quarles

Usually when people are sad, they don't do anything... But when they get angry, they bring about a change.

—Malcolm X (El-Hajj Malik El-Shabazz)

Great thoughts reduced to practice become great acts.

—William Hazlitt

Don't watch the clock; do what it does. Keep going.

—Sam Levenson

Actions speak louder than words.

—English language proverb

The actions of men are the best interpreters of their thoughts.

—John Locke

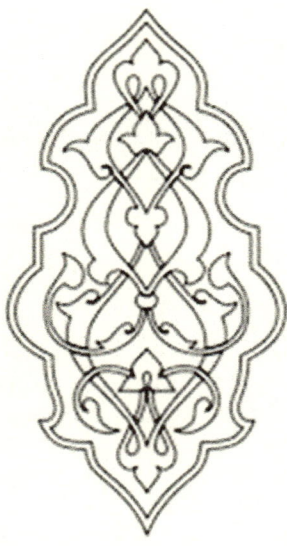

Advice

Advice | Eastern

And speak unto him a gentle word.

—Qur'an 20:44

The deaf are those who do not listen to good advice.

—South Asian proverb

If your words are worthless, don't give advice.

—Chinese proverb

Most caring help is to give good advice.

—Persian proverb

Take it from me, do not advise too much; do the job yourself.

—Jawaharlal Nehru

It is unprofitable to hammer cold iron. [No use giving advice to those who will not listen.]

—Persian proverb

Give thine ear, and hear what I say, and apply thine heart to apprehend; It is good for thee to place them in thine heart, let them rest in the casket of thy belly; That they may act as a peg upon thy tongue.

—Amenemope
Quoted in The Legacy of Egypt

Support me with your advice in private, and avoid advising me in public.

—Al-Shafi 'i

The general that hearkens to my counsel and acts upon it, will conquer.!

—Sun Tzu

Beware of unsolicited advice.

—The Talmud

Suppose me a steel weapon, I will use you for a whetstone: suppose me a year of drought, I will use you for a copious rain.

—Chinese

Stubbornness destroys (good) advice.

> —Ali (Ali ibn Abi Talib)
> *Nahj al-Balagha (Peak of Eloquence)*

The truths we least wish to hear are those which is most to our advantage to know.

> —Chinese proverb

Advice | Western

When your mother asks, "Do you want a piece of advice?" it is a mere formality. It doesn't matter if you answer yes or no. You're going to get it anyway.

> —Erma Louise (Harris) Bombeck

How can they advise, if they see but a part?

> —Benjamin Franklin

No enemy is worse than bad advice.

> —Sophocles

Gildor: Seldom give unguarded advice, for advice is a dangerous gift, even from the wise to the wise, and all courses may run ill.

> —J. R. R. Tolkien

Advice is not a popular thing to give.

> —Disraeli

Fools need Advice most, but wise Men only are the better for it.

> —Benjamin Franklin

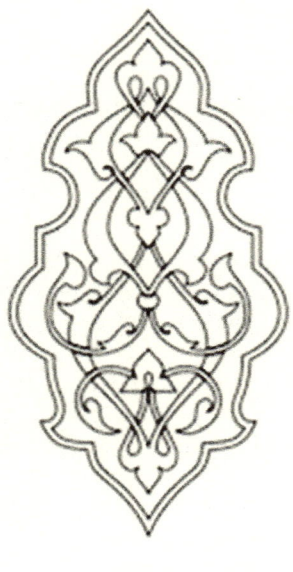

Age

Age | Eastern

In the young century's cool nursery,
In its chequered silence, I was born.

—Anna Akhmatova
Willow

The aged forget; the young don't know.

—Japanese proverb

Youth is wasted on the young.

—South Asian proverb

Is there any joy as pure and sorrow as fleeting as that of childhood.

—Mulk Raj Anand
Seven Summer

I find a lot in common in the way I manage things [as Director General of the International Atomic Energy Agency (IAEA)] and the way she [his wife, a kindergarten teacher] manages three-year olds. We humans are the same when we are three years old and when we are 50!

—Mohamed ElBaradei
"Breaking the Cycle," Cairo Times, October 23, 2003

It is not by living long, but by seeing much, that one learns.

—Turkish proverb

To honor an old man is showing respect to God.

—Muhammad
Quoted in Al-Suhrawardy, The Sayings of Muhammad

Age | Western

As a white candle in a holy place, so is the beauty of an aged face.
—Joseph Campbell
Irish Poem, "The Old Woman"

Age is a question of mind over matter. If you don't mind, age don't matter.
—Leroy "Satchel" Paige

A young tree bends, and old tree breaks.
—Yiddish proverb

By the time your eighty years old you've learned everything. You only have to remember it.
—George Burns

You can't teach old dogs new tricks.
—English language proverb

Old age takes away from us what we have inherited and gives us what we have earned.
—Gerald Brenan

Rumble, young man, rumble!
—Muhammad Ali (Cassius Clay)

Not by age but by capacity is wisdom acquired.
—Plautus (Titus Maccius Plautus)

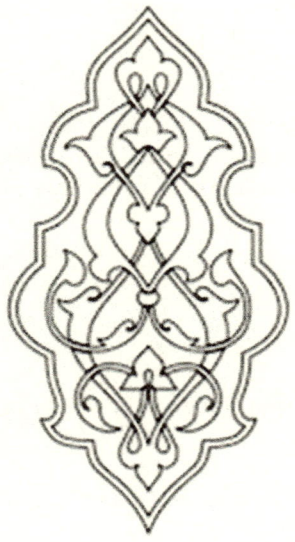

Ambition

Ambition | Eastern

Aut viam inveniam aut faciam.
I will either find a way, or make one.

—Hannibal

Attributed. Salesmanship and Business Efficiency It is the privilege of man to work for fruits that are beyond his immediate reach.

—Rabindranath Tagore

Dwell not upon thy weariness, thy strength shall be according to the measure of thy desire.

—Arabic proverb

When we learn from the West, it is evident that we should learn the latest inventions instead of repeating the different steps of development... In this way we can easily within ten years catch up with the West in material achievement.

—Sun Yat-sen
1924 speech, The World's Great Speeches

Ambition is bondage.

—Ibn Gabirol

One who is in search of something will obtain it, (or) at least part.

—Ali (Ali ibn Abi Talib)

Man shall have nothing but what he strives for.

—Qur'an 53:39

Ambition | Western

Someday I shall be President.

—Abraham Lincoln

In man, ambition is common'st thing;
Each one, by nature, loves to be a king.

—Robert Herrick
The Poetical Works of Robert Herrick

Keep away from people who try to belittle your ambitions. Small people always do that, but the really great make you feel that you, too, can become great.
—Mark Twain (Samuel L. Clemens)

Brutus: As he was valiant, I honor him; but as he was ambitious, I slew him.
—Shakespeare
Julius Caesar

Hitch your wagon to a star.

—Ralph Waldo Emerson

Vain the ambition of kings
Who seek by trophies and dead things
To leave a living name behind,
And weave but nets to catch the wind.

—John Webster

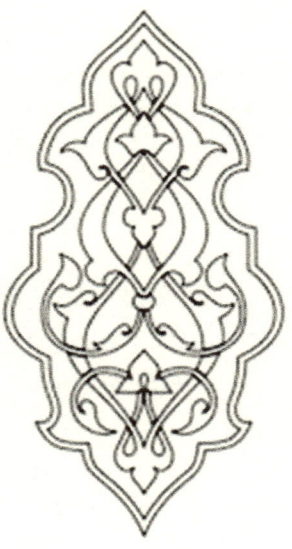

Art and Artist

Art and Artist | Eastern

Science and art are servants of life,
Slaves born and bred in its house.

—Iqbal (Sir Muhammad Iqbal)

The purpose of art is to impart the sensation of things as they are perceived and not as they are known.

—Viktor Borisovich Shklovsky

Art as Technique

Art is a faithful mirror of life and civilization of a period.

—Jawaharlal Nehru

We cannot fail to observe that art is one of the means of effective communication between people.

—Leo Tolstoy

Art arises when the secret vision of the artist and the manifestation of nature agree to find new shapes.

—Kahlil Gibran
The Kahlil Gibran Reader: Inspirational Writings

Art and Artist | Western

I paint my own reality.

—Frida Kahlo

The artist is not a reporter, but a Great Teacher. It is not his business to depict the world as it is, but as it ought to be.

—H. L. Mencken
"The Greenwich Village Complex," American Mercury, June, 1925

Art is a marriage of the conscious and unconscious.

—Jean Cocteau

Life is art. It unfolds itself step by step, breath by breath.

—Anthony J. Manha

Art is the reproduction of what the senses perceive in nature through the veil of the soul.

—Edgar Allan Poe

The true artist sees the harmony, the wholeness, the tendencies toward perfection in things everywhere.

—Guggenheimer

It is art, and art only, that reveals us to ourselves.

—Oscar Wilde

Let each man exercise the art he knows.

—Aristophanes

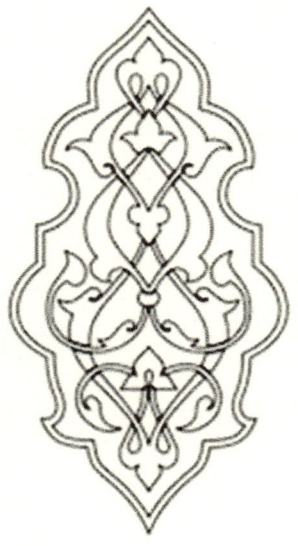

Beauty

Beauty | Eastern

Verily God is beautiful and loves beauty.

—Muhammad

Sahih al-Bukhari

Everything has its beauty but not everyone sees it.
—Confucius (K'ung-Fu-Tzu)

O beauty, so ancient and so new!
—St. Augustine of Hippo

I have become so feeble that to kill me
It is quite enough for the beauty to fl ick the sword of her brows.
—Ghani

The mind needs to relax by contemplating pictures and other beautiful objects.
—Maimonides

Beauty is eternity gazing at itself in a mirror.
—Kahlil Gibran

Beauty is indeed a good gift of God; but that the good may not think it a great good, God dispenses it even to the wicked.
—St. Augustine of Hippo

Beauty will save the world.
—Fyodor Dostoyevski

It is amazing how complete is the delusion that beauty is goodness.
—Leo Tolstoy

Everything on earth [is] beautiful, everything, except what we ourselves think and do when we forget the higher purposes of life and our own human dignity.
—Anton Chekhov
The Lady with the Toy Dog, trans. Koteliansky and Cannan

Do you sell roses? But the question is:
What are you then going to buy finer than roses?
Even if the buyer is more generous than the king,
All the same you would not make any profit.

—Kisai Marvazi

Quoted in Natalia Prigarina, Mirza Ghalib: A Creative Biography

Go the road upon which no foot-track is,
View the beauty that transcends all vision;
Learn the knowledge speech cannot tell.

—Nisami

Lust not after her beauty in thine heart; neither let her take thee with her eyelids.

—Proverbs 6:25

Beauty | Western

A thing of beauty is a joy for ever:
Its loveliness increases; it will never
Pass into nothingness.

—John Keats
Endymion, 1818

Doth perfect beauty stand in need of praise at all? Nay; no more than law, no more than truth, no more than loving kindness, nor than modesty.

—Marcus T. Cicero

[The beautiful] is that which please us when they are seen.

—St. Thomas Aquinas

The best and most beautiful things in the world cannot be seen or even touched. They must be felt with the heart.

—Helen Keller

Beauty is the purgation of superfluities.

—Michelangelo

Quoted in Emerson, The Conduct of Life
Beauty can inspire miracles.

—Disraeli

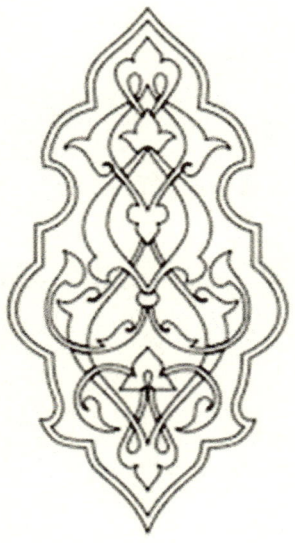

Being

Being | Eastern

Being unconquerable lies within yourself.

—Sun Tzu

We all have two mirrors, one inside and the other external.
—Abul Kalam Azad
Quoted in Eight Lives: A Study of the Hindu-Muslim Encounter

What is this precious love and laughter
Budding in our hearts?
It is the glorious sound
Of a soul waking up!
—Hafiz (Shamsu d-Din Muhammad Hafiz)
Quoted in Daniel Ladinsky, The Gift: Poems by Hafiz the Great Sufi Master

A journey of thousands starts with a single step.

—Lao Tzu

The more isolated a person is from the "native" self the more (s)he takes on the image of the other.

—Alamin M. Mazrui
The Power of Babel: Language and Governance in the African Experience

Do you think that you are some small mass
While within you there dwells a great world?

—Ali
Quoted in Al-Kashani, M. M., Tafsir al-Safi

Having drunk entire seas, we remain quite surprised that our lips are just as dry as the shore, and we continue to seek out the sea to dip them there, without seeing that our lips are the shore and we ourselves the sea.

—Attar (Farid al-Din Attar)
Conference of the Birds

Take one step away from yourself—and behold!—the path!
—Abu Sa'id (Abu Sa'id ibn Abi'l-Khayr)

There are men who are chained to gold and silver.

—The Talmud

[The self is] the wakefulness of creation,
the inner mystery of life

—Iqbal
Bal-e-Jibril (Wings of Gabriel)

If out of the three hundred Songs I had to take one phrase to cover all my teachings, I would say, "Let there be no evil in your [private] thoughts."

—Confucius

Why should I ask the wise men: Whence is my beginning?... I am busy with the thought: What will be my end.?

—Iqbal

The well-being of the soul can only be obtained after that of the body has been secured.

—Moses Maimonides

Being | Western

Do I contradict myself?
Very well then... I contradict myself;
I am large... I contain multitudes.

—Walt Whitman
"Song of Myself," Leaves of Grass

Two souls, alas, are housed within my breast,
And each will wrestle for the mastery there.

—Goethe
Faust, 1

Seek... thyself!

—Miguel de Unamuno
Tragic Sense of Life, 10, 1913, trans. J. E. Crawford Flitch, 1921

I think the king is but a man as I am; the violet smells to him as it doth to me.

—Shakespeare
Henry V

31

Many men go fishing all of their lives without knowing that it is not fish they are after.

—Henry David Thoreau

There seemed to be two pleading in me.

—George Fox

The Journal of George Fox, 1694

One does not know that one exists until one rediscovers oneself in others.

—Goethe
Letter to August Stolberg, 13 February 1775

Conscious and unconscious are not necessarily in opposition to one another, but complement one another to form a totality, which is the self.

—Carl G. Jung
"The Relations between the Ego and the Unconscious" (2.1), 1928,
Two Essays on Analytical Psychology, trans. R. F. C. Hull, 1953

There is a deep disorder in our society which comes not from the machinations of our enemies and from the adversities of the human condition but from within ourselves.

—Walter Lippman
The Public Philosophy, 1.1, 1955

"A battle is raging inside me… it is a terrible fight between two wolves. One wolf represents fear, anger, envy, sorrow, regret, greed, arrogance, self-pity, guilt, resentment, inferiority, lies, false pride, superiority and ego. The other stands for joy, peace, love, hope, sharing, serenity, humility, kindness, benevolence, friendship, empathy, generosity, truth, compassion and faith."

The old man fixed the children with a firm stare. "This same fight is going on inside you, and inside every other person, too."

They thought about it for a minute and then one child asked his grand-father, "Which wolf will win?"

The old Cherokee replied: "The one you feed."

—Cherokee Tradition

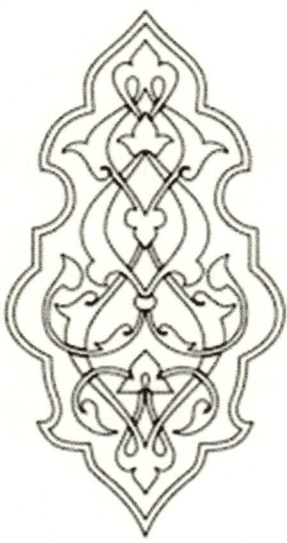

Boldness

Boldness | Eastern

And thou, brave heart, arise. Be free of every chain, though blazing with gold.
Be nobly bold. Follow the true bride of thy life, though her name be Sorrow.

—Rumi
Quoted in Pebbles, Pearls and Gems of the Orient, 1882

Consume my sorrows by that flood whose taste
Would urge the lion to lay forests waste.
Heaven let me master as a lion bold,
And rend the net of Time, that wolf so old.

—Hafiz
Quoted in Pebbles, Pearls and Gems of the Orient

Boldness | Western

MacBeth: I dare do all that [I] may become a man;
Who dares do more is none.

—Shakespeare
Macbeth

Tell them, it was because he was too bold!
And told those truths, which should not have been told!

—Daniel Defoe

Take calculated risks. That is quite different from being rash.

—George S. Patton Jr.

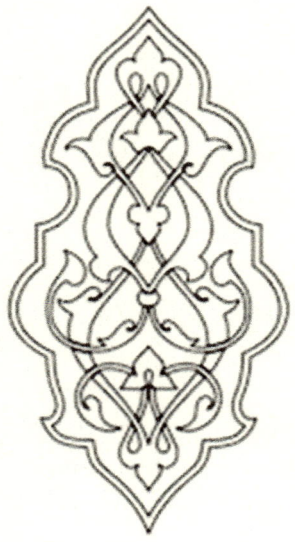

Caution

Caution | Eastern

The cautious seldom err.

—Confucius
The Analects

Safety is in caution, and regret is in haste.

—Arabic proverb

The tree that has only just taken root may be pulled up by the strength of a man; but should it continue some time in that state, it could not be eradicated even by a windlass.

—Sa'di

Caution | Western

Hasten slowly.

—Caesar Augustus

Be wary then; best safety lies in fear.

—Shakespeare
Hamlet

The torment of precautions often exceeds the dangers to be avoided. It is sometimes better to abandon one's self to destiny.

—Napoleon Bonaparte

Change and Progress

Change and Progress | Eastern

Fixed formation is bad. Study this well.

—Miyamoto Musashi
Go Rin No Sho (The Book of Five Rings), 1645

There is nothing like returning to a place that remains unchanged to find the ways in which you yourself have altered.

—Nelson Mandela

Change is inevitable, but it is in us to control its content and direction.

—Indira Gandhi

We need to be the change we wish to see in the world.

—Mahatma Gandhi

Verily never will God change the condition of a people until they change themselves.

—Qur'an 13:11

It is only the wisest and the very stupidest who cannot change.

—Confucius

Who will change old lamps for new ones?

—One Thousand and One Nights
"The History of Aladdin"

Ignorance is always afraid of change.

—Jawaharlal Nehru

Change and Progress | Western

No man ever steps in the same river twice, for it's not the same river and he's not the same man.

—Heraclitus

We must always change, renew, rejuvenate ourselves; otherwise we harden.

—Goethe

Progress is impossible without change; and those who cannot change their minds cannot change anything.

—George Bernard Shaw

The more things change, the more they stay the same.

—Alphonse Karr

Never underestimate your power to change yourself; never overestimate your power to change others.

—H. Jackson Brown Jr.
Life's Little Instruction Book, items 284-285, 1991

I find the great thing in this world is not so much where we stand, as in what direction we are moving.

—Oliver Wendell Holmes

"Future shock"... [is] the shattering stress and disorientation that we induce in individuals by subjecting them to too much change in too short a time.

—Alvin Toffler

If you want to make enemies, try to change something.

—Woodrow Wilson

Nought endures but change.

—Boerne, Memorial Address on Jean Paul

Nothing endures but change.

—Heraclitus

Everything subject to time is liable to change.

—Rabbi Joseph Albo

We cannot change anything until we accept it.

—Carl Gustav Jung

We believe that the most basic of all changes in human social organization have been the result of three processes. Starting 8,000 to 10,000 years ago, agriculture was invented in the Middle East— probably by a woman. That's the First Wave. Roughly 250 years ago, the Industrial Revolution triggered a Second Wave of change. Brute force technologies amplified human and animal muscle power and gave rise to an urban, factory-centered way of life. Sometime after World War II, a gigantic Third Wave began transforming the planet, based on tools that amplify mind rather than muscle. The Third Wave is bigger, deeper and faster than the other two.

—Alvin Toffler

Claudia Dreifus interview with Toffler and Heidi Toffler,
"Present Shock," New York Times Magazine, June 11, 1995

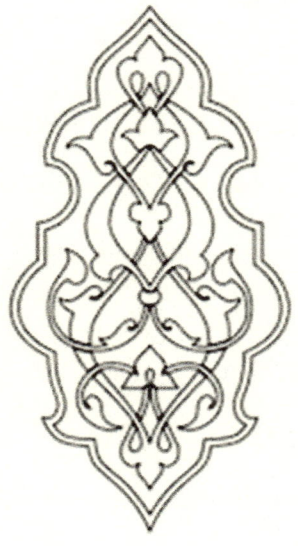

Character, Virtue, and Conduct

Character, Virtue, and Conduct | Eastern

When a character of a man is not clear to you, look at his friends.
—Japanese proverb

Improve your own conduct before asking others to improve theirs.
—Abu Bakr
In Ghulam Sarwar, Islam Beliefs and Teachings

To be aware of a single shortcoming in oneself is more useful than to be aware of a thousand in someone else.
—Dalai Lama

The virtues are not poured into us, they are natural.
Seek, and you will find them: neglect, and you will lose them.
—Mencius
Quoted in Pebbles, Pearls and Gems of the Orient, 1882

The best of people are those with the most excellent character.
—Muhammad
Sahih Tabarâni

Unity of thought without unity of conduct is an empty dream!
—Iqbal
Zarb-i-Kalim

Your character is really your beauty and not your looks.
—Nigerian adage

Do not judge a person only by his performance of Salah (prayers) and Sawm (fasting); rather look into his truthfulness and wisdom.
—Umar
In Ghulam Sarwar, Islam Beliefs and Teachings

Virtue is the key to success.
—Ali
In Ghulam Sarwar, Islam Beliefs and Teachings

Virtue never lacks company; it will ever find support.
—Chinese proverb

O' my son, learn four things from me. Nothing will harm you if you practice them. That the riches is intelligence; the biggest destitution is foolishness; the wildest wildness is vanity and the best achievement is goodness of the moral character.

—Ali
Nahj al-Balagha (Peak of Eloquence)

The superior man thinks of virtue; the small man thinks of comfort.

—Confucius
The Analects

Good humor and character is manifested in a cheerful face, generous giving, and not imposing one's problems on others.

—Hassan al-Basri

Character, not brain, will count at the crucial moment.

—Rabindranath Tagore

Character, virtue, and Conduct | Western

We will be known by the tracks we leave behind.

—Dakota proverb

I can tolerate the fool bettr than him who is wise in his own eyes.

—Berechiah ha-Nakdan

It is not in the still calm of life, or the repose of a pacific station, that great characters are formed… Great necessities call out great virtues.

—Abigail Adams

Character is formed in the stormy billows of the world.

—Goethe

Virtue is choked with foul ambition.

—Shakespeare
Dictionary of Burning Words of Brilliant Writers

Character is what you are in the dark.

—Dwight L. Moody

People always say they are not themselves when tempted by anger into betraying what they really are.

—Ed Howe

Character is destiny.

—Heraclitus

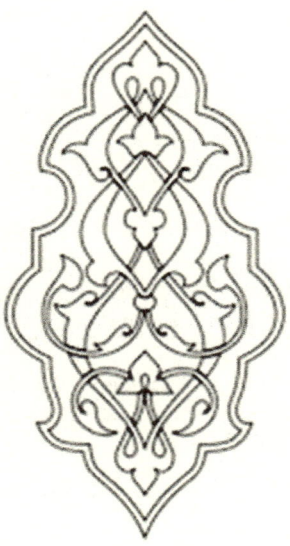

Circumstances

Circumstances | Eastern

Through change of circumstances the mettle of men is known.

—Ali
Nahj al-Balagha (Peak of Eloquence)

A wise man adapts to circumstances just as water shapes itself to the vessel that contains it.

—Chinese proverb

Strong winds are blowing all over Asia. Let us not be afraid.

—Jawaharlal Nehru
The World's Great Speeches

If the whole world were swallowed by the sea,
what would it matter to the duck?

—Shams of Tabriz
Rumi's Sun: The Teachings of Shams of Tabriz, 2008

On every side is an ambush laid by the robber troops of circumstance.
Hence it is that the horseman of life urges on his courser at headlong speed.

—Hafiz
Quoted in Pebbles, pearls and gems of the Orient

Circumstances | Western

Circumstances are the rulers of the weak; they are but the instruments of the wise.

—Samuel Lover

The same wind that carries one vessel into port, may blow another off shore.

—C. N. Bovee

The meeting of two personalities is like the contact of two chemical substances: if there is any reaction, both are transformed.

—Carl Gustav Jung

You must sail according to the wind.

—Piconnerie de la Bugeaud

What is the matter with the world that it is so out of joint? Simply that men do not rule themselves but let circumstances rule them.

—Ralph Waldo Emerson

Circumstances reveal us to others and still more to ourselves.

—La Rochefoucauld

To each circumstance its own law.

—Napoleon Bonaparte

In the very circumstance of dispersion may lie fulfillment.

—D. Kaufmann

Civilization

Civilization | Eastern

A civilization is to be judged by its treatment of minorities.
—Mahatma Gandhi (1869-1948)
Quoted in The Life of Mahatma Gandhi, 1950

I do not believe that civilizations, by definition, can clash. What we have between East and West is not a "clash" of civilizations, or of religions, but a situation bred by politics because of perceptions...
—Ahmed Zewail
Interview with Aziza Sami, "Clash of Words,
Al-Ahram Weekly Online, no. 573, February 14-20, 2002

We must recognize that it is providential that the West has come to India. And yet some one must show the East to the West, and convince the West that the East has her contribution to make to the history of civilization.
—Rabindranath Tagore
1925 speech, The World's Great Speeches

The hand of God is upon the majority [of the community].
—Muhammad
Tirmidhi (a book of prophetic traditions)

Social organization... is necessary to the human species.
—Ibn Khaldun
The Muqaddimah: An Introduction to History

A basic change in political ethics is required for the realization of the [dialogue among civilizations].
—Mohammad Khatami
Address, UNESCO, 1999

The World is held up by four pillars:
The Wisdom of the Learned
The Justice of the Great
The Prayers of the Righteous and
The Valor of the Brave.

—Inscription at the entrance of
University of Granada in former Muslim Spain

While civilization is the body, culture is the soul; while civilization is the result of knowledge and great painful researches in diverse fields, culture is the result of wisdom.

—Shri Prakash

Civilizations, like empires, fall, not so much because of the strength of the enemy, as through the weakness and decay within.

—Jawaharlal Nehru

I speak bitterly of Western civilization when I am conscious that it is betraying its trust and thwarting its own purpose. The West must not make herself a curse to the world by using her power for her own selfish needs, but, by teaching the ignorant and helping the weak.

—Rabindranath Tagore
1925 speech, The World's Great Speeches

Life of the individual depends on the body and soul.
Life of a nation depends on the preservation of its tradition and culture. An individual dies if the life-flow ceases. A nation dies if the ideals of its people are ignored!

—Iqbal
Quoted in Almajiri and Qur'anic Education

Civilization | Western

Is it progress if a cannibal uses knife and fork?

—Stanislaus J. Lec

Civilizations are born out of the pursuit of luxury.

—Bertrand Russell

Increased means and increased leisure are the two civilizers of man.

—Disraeli

I do believe that there will be a clash between East and West. I believe that there will be a clash between those who want freedom, justice and equality for everyone and those who want to continue the systems of exploitation. I believe that there will be that kind of clash, but I don't think that it will be based upon the color of the skin.
—Malcolm X (El-Hajj Malik El-Shabazz)
Malcolm X Speaks, 1965

Without books the development of civilization would have been impossible. They are the engines of change, windows on the world, "Lighthouses" as the poet said "erected in the sea of time." They are companions, teachers, magicians, bankers of the treasures of the mind. Books are humanity in print.
—Arthur Schopenhauer

Civilization is a movement and not a condition, a voyage and not a harbour. It is the sum total of all progress made by man in every sphere of action and from every point of view in so far as the progress helps towards the spiritual perfecting of individuals as the progress of all progress.
—Albert Schweitzer
The Philosophy of Civilization

Not only the individual advances from infancy to manhood, but the species itself from rudeness to civilization.
—Adam Ferguson
An Essay on the History of Civil Society, 1767

[Civilization is] the highest cultural grouping of people and the broadest level of cultural identity people have short of that which distinguishes humans from other species.
—Samuel Phillips Huntington

Necessity and virtue create a civilization, while indulgence and vice work to tear it down.

—Anonymous

Civilizations die from suicide, not by murder.

—Arnold Toynbee

Civilization begins with order, grows with liberty, dies with chaos.

—Will Durant

[On ancient Athens]: In the end, more than freedom, they wanted security. They wanted a comfortable life, and they lost it all—security, comfort, and freedom. When the Athenians finally wanted not to give to society but for society to give to them, when the freedom they wished for most was freedom from responsibility, then Athens ceased to be free and was never free again.

—Edward Gibbon

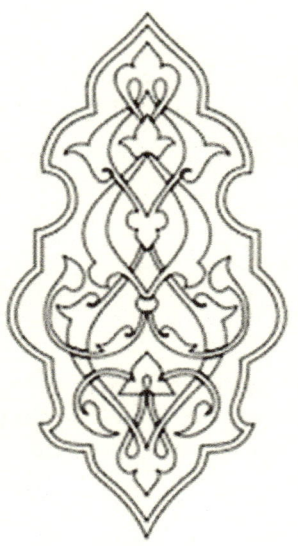

Critique

Critique | Eastern

el-faDi ye3mel 'aDi
He who isn't busy acts like a judge.

—Arabic proverb

They found no wrong with the roses, so they complain it's too red!

—Egyptian proverb

A man's mind is hidden in his writings; criticism brings it to light.

—Ibn Gabirol

The government needs criticism from its people... Without this criticism the government will not be able to function... We must learn from old mistakes, take all forms of healthy criticism.

—Zhou Enlai
1956 speech

Throughout my life I have gained more from my critic friends than from my admirers.

—Mahatma Gandhi

"One of the most heinous acts is for a person to curse his parents," to which someone asked how one could stoop to cursing their own parents, he replied, "He curses the father of another man and in retort the other person curses his own father and mother."

—Muhammad
Sahih al-Bukhari (a book of prophetic traditions)

Critique | Western

To escape criticism, do nothing, say nothing, be nothing.

—Elbert Hubbard

The critics are sentinels in the grand army of letters.

—Henry W. Longfellow

So long as I am acting from duty and conviction, I am indifferent to taunts. I think they will probably do me more good than harm.

—Winston Churchill
House of Commons speech, December 6, 1946

It is much easier to be critical than to be correct.

—Benjamin Disraeli
House of Commons speech, January 24, 1860

The sting of a reproach is the truth of it.

—Thomas Fuller
Gnomologia: Adages and Proverbs, no. 4769, 1732

You can spot a bad critic when he starts by discussing the poet and not the poem.

—Ezra Pound
In Naomi Rachel, letter to New Yorker, December 25, 1995

I don't pay much attention to critics. The world is divided into two kinds of people: those who can, and those who criticize.

—Ronald Reagan
In Michael Korda, "Prompting the President," New Yorker, October 6, 1997

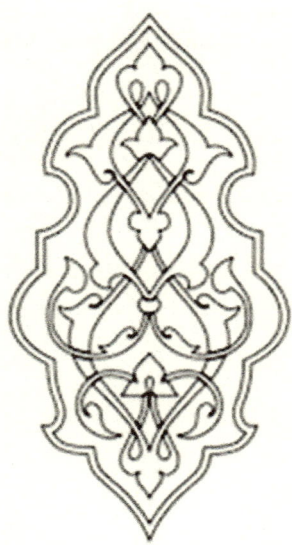

Culture

Culture | Eastern

Culturally, there are many "Easts" and many "Wests" and they are by no means all necessarily irreconcilable.

—Peng Chun Chang
China at the Crossroads: The Chinese Situation in Perspective

A nation's culture resides in the heart and in the soul of its people.

—Mahatma Gandhi

Education which poses a neutral attitude towards culture and ideals of the society, will act as a force of disintegration and destroy the social fabric of the society.

—Khurshid Ahmad
Principles of Islamic Education, 1984

White people have often confused the symbol of our poverty with our culture.

—Tom Mboya

Culture | Western

[Culture is the] pursuit of our total perfection.

—Matthew Arnold

Culture and Anarchy, 1869; emphasis added

Culture is the sum of all the forms of art, of love and of thought, which, in the course of centuries, have enabled man to be less enslaved.

—André Malraux

Whoever controls the media—the images—controls the culture.

—Allen Ginsberg

For whatever else education may mean, it must mean primarily the self-perpetuation of an accepted culture—a culture which is the life of a determined society.

—Professor Clarke

Culture is always a product of mixing.

—F. Hertz

Culture may even be described simply as that which makes life worth living.

—T. S. Elliot

The value of culture is its effect on character. It avails nothing unless it ennobles and strengthens that. Its use is for life. Its aim is not beauty but goodness.

—W. Somerset Maugham

Discovery and Exploration

Discovery and Exploration | Eastern

Darkness within darkness.
The gate to all mystery.

—Lao Tzu
Tao Te Ching

I have wandered to various regions of the world, and everywhere have I mixed freely with the inhabitants. I have gathered something in each corner. I have gleaned an ear from every harvest.

—Sa'di
Sadi's Scroll of Wisdom

Learn a new flight, learn a new sight
get up from your deep sleep

—Iqbal
Zabur-i-Ajam (Persian Psalms), 1927

Strange—is it not?—that, of the myriads who
Before us passed the door of darkness through,
Not one returns to tell us of the road
Which, to discover, we must travel too.

—Omar Khayyam
Quoted in The Rubaiyat of Omar Khayyam, trans. Fitzgerald

It is within man's province to explore all things...

—Dunash Ibn Tamim
Commentary to Servery Yetzira

Discovery and Exploration | Western

Discovery consists in seeing what everybody has seen and thinking what nobody has thought.

—Albert Szent-Györgyi
Bioenergetics, 1957

The greatest obstacle to discovery is not ignorance—it is the illusion of knowledge.

—Daniel J. Boorstin
In Carol Krucor, "The 6 o'Clock Scholar," Washington Post, January 29, 1984

No great discovery was ever made in science except by one who lifted his nose above the grindstone of details and ventured on a more comprehensive vision.

—Albert Einstein
In Morris R. Cohen, The Meaning of Human History, 6.4, 1947

Although the envious nature of men, so prompt to blame and so slow to praise, makes the discovery and introduction of any new principles and systems as dangerous almost as the exploration of unknown seas and continents.

—Machiavelli
Discourses on Titus Livius, Book I

Divine

Divine | Eastern

Whenever you contain Him in your imagination and whim, he will not be Allah (God) but a creation like yourself and revertible towards you.

—Imam al-Baqir

Man's love of God is identical with his knowledge of Him.

—Moses Maimonides

The net of heaven is very wide in its meshes, and yet it misses nothing.

—Lao Tzu

Verily God is beautiful and loves beauty.

—Muhammad

All things but God are contingent; only He is a Necessary Being.

—Avicenna
Attributed. Lenn Evan Goodman, Avicenna

I asked the earth and it answered me: "I am not it," and all things made the same confession. I asked the sea and the deeps and the creeping things and they answered me: "We are not thy God; seek beyond us."

—St. Augustine of Hippo

Caress the detail, the divine detail.

—Vladimir Nabokov

My God, my dearest thought is remembrance of you, the sweetest word on my tongue is praise of you, and my dearest hour is the hour I meet you.

—Yahya ibn Mu'adh

Do His will as if it were your own, so that He will do His will as it were yours. Nullify your own will before His so that he will nul-lify the will of others before you.

—Pirkei Avot

God is, even though the whole world deny him.

—Mohandas Gandhi

Praise be to God,
The Cherisher and Sustainer of the worlds;
Most Gracious, Most Merciful;
Master of the Day of Judgment.
Thee do we worship,
And Thine aid we seek.
Show us the straight way,
The way of those on whom
Thou hast bestowed Thy Grace,
Those whose (portion)
Is not wrath,
And who go not astray.

—Qur'an, Sura 1

In the name of God, stop a moment, cease your work, look around you.
—Leo Tolstoy

A group of people worshipped God out of desire for reward surely, this is the worship of traders. Another worshipped God out of fear, this is the worship of slaves. Still another worshipped God out of gratefulness, this is the worship of free men.

—Ali

God judged it better to bring good out of evil than to suffer no evil to exist.
—Saint Augustine

If the "ulama" (faithful scholars) are not God's friends, then God has no friends in the world.

—Abu Hanifa

Within the Kaaba (house of God), there is no *qiblah*
(direction of prayer),
Outside the Kaaba, one must find the *qiblah*.

—Shams of Tabriz

Man 'arafa nafsahu faqad 'arafa Rabbahu.
Whosoever knows himself knows his Lord.

—Ibn Arabia

Divine | Western

I don't believe. I know.

—Carl Jung
When asked if he believed in God. In "The Old Wise Man," Time, February, 14, 1955

Hier stehe ich. Ich kann nicht Anders tun. Gott hilfe mir. Amen!
Here I stand; I can do no otherwise. God help me. Amen!

—Martin Luther
Speech at the Diet of Worms, 1521

God was a mathematician whose calculations, although infinite in their subtle complexity, were accessible to man's intelligence.

—Isaac Newton
In Norman Hampson, The Enlightenment, 1976

We have one life; it soon will be past; what we do for God is all that will last.

—Muhammad Ali

The love that moves the sun and the other stars.

—Dante Alighieri
Paradiso, XXXIII, 1320

In the endless self-repeating
For evermore flows the same.
Myriad arches springing, meeting,
Hold at rest the mighty frame.
Streams from all things love of living,
Grandes star and humblest cold,
All the straining, all the striving
Is eternal peace in God."

—Goethe
Quoted in Goethe. Gedichte, hg. und kommentiert v. Erich Trunz, München, 1974

Man has a dual citizenry. He lives both in time and in eternity; both in heaven and on earth. Be he owes his ultimate allegiance to God.

—Martin Luther King Jr.
Stride Toward Freedom

I have felt His hand upon me in great trials and submitted to His guidance, and I trust that as He shall further open the way, I will be ready to walk therein, relying on His help and trusting in His goodness and wisdom.

—Abraham Lincoln
Remark to a White House visitor, June 1862. In James F. Wilson,
North America Review, December 1896

By God's grace, I know Satan very well. If Satan can turn God's Word upside down and pervert the Scriptures, what will he do with my words—or the words of others?

—Martin Luther
Confession Concerning Christ's Supper

Nature is but a name for an effect,
Whose cause is God.

—William Cowper
The Task, 6.223, 1785

The use of nature is to awaken the feeling of the absolute... It is the shadow pointing to an unseen sun.

—Ralph Waldo Emerson
Journal, April 7, 1836

For man proposes, but God disposes.

—Thomas A. Kempis
Imitation of Christ

It is impossible to account for the creation of the universe without the agency of a Supreme Being.

—George Washington
In James K. Paulding, The Life of Washington, 1848

I have concluded the evident existence of God, and that my existence depends entirely on God in all the moments of my life, that I do not think that the human spirit may know anything with greater evidence and certitude.

—René Descartes
"Les Meditations," The Meditations and Selections from the Principles of René
Descartes, 1950

The world embarrasses me, and I cannot dream... That this watch exists and has no watchmaker.

—Voltaire

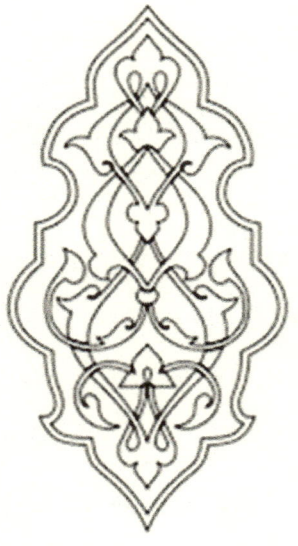

Doubt and Fear

Doubt and Fear | Eastern

Deep roots fear no wind.

—Chinese proverb

My mind is the battlefield of my life
Where there are armies of doubts
but where conviction is steadfast

—Iqbal
Iqbal: Poet-Philosopher of Islam

At the bottom of great doubt lies great awakening.

—Hakuin Ekaku

I learned that courage was not the absence of fear, but the triumph over it.

—Nelson Mandela
Long Walk to Freedom

The world perishes then in the night of its doubt.

—Mahmud Ferjumendi
Quoted in Pebbles, Pearls and Gems of the Orient, no. 671, 1882

Do not turn your knowledge into ignorance or your conviction into doubt.

—Ali
Nahj al-Balagha (Peak of Eloquence)

You can win by making best use of the enemy's frightened rhythm.

—Miyamoto Musashi

Doubt and Fear | Western

A man with one watch knows what time it is; a man with two watches is never quite sure.

—Lee Segall

If the sun and moon should doubt,
They'd immediately go out.

—William Blake
"Auguries of Innocence," The Pickering Manuscript

Doubt is the beginning, not the end of wisdom.

—George Henry

It is part of the general pattern of misguided policy that our country is now geared to an arms economy which was bred in an artificially induced psychosis of war hysteria and nurtured upon an incessant propaganda of fear.

—General Douglas MacArthur
Speech, May 15, 1951

Doubt grows with knowledge.

—Goethe
Sprüche in Prosa

If a man will begin with certainties, he shall end in doubts; but if he will be content to begin with doubts, he shall end in certainties.

—Francis Bacon
The Advancement of Learning, 1605

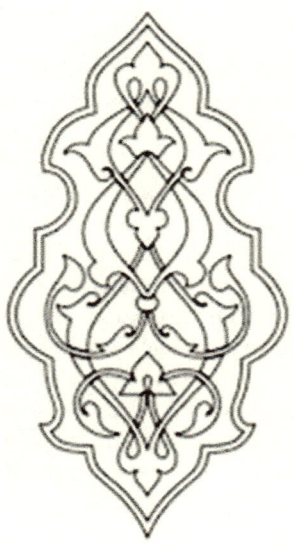

Economics

Economics | Eastern

Where the army is, prices are high; when prices rise the wealth of the people is exhausted.

—Sun Tzu

Poverty has been created by the economic and social systems that we have designed for the world. It is the institutions that we have built, and feel so proud of, which created poverty.

—Muhammad Yunus
Global Urban Development Magazine, May 2005

There must be an end to white monopoly on political power and a fundamental restructuring of our political and economic systems to ensure that the inequalities of apartheid are addressed.

—Nelson Mandela
Address to Rally in Cape Town on his release from prison

In the early stages of the state, taxes are light, but fetch in a large revenue... As time passes and kings succeed each other, they lose their tribal habits in favor of more civilized ones. Their needs and exigencies grow... owing to the luxury in which they have been brought up. Hence they impose fresh taxes on their subjects... [&] sharply raise the rate of old taxes to increase their yield... But the effects on business of this rise in taxation make themselves felt. For business men are soon discouraged by the comparison of their profits with the burden of their taxes... Consequently production falls off, and with it the yield of taxation.

—Ibn Khaldun
Note: In economics, this is known as the Khaldun-Laffer Curve
(the relationship between tax rates and tax revenue follows an inverted U shape)

Economics | Western

We might come closer to balancing the budget if all of us lived closer to the Commandments and the Golden Rule.

—Ronald Reagan

If all economists were laid end to end, they would not reach a conclusion.

—George Bernard Shaw

The economic system is the foundation on which the political superstructure is erected.

—Lenin
The Three Sources and Three Component Parts of Marxism, 1913

Beware of the little expenses, a small leak will sink a great ship.

—Benjamin Franklin

The great virtue of a free market system is that it does not care what color people are; it does not care what their religion is; it only cares whether they can produce something you want to buy.

—Milton Friedman

On money: Save it when you need it least. Spend it when you have it most.

—Franco Modiglani

It is a recession when your neighbor loses his job; it's a depression when you lose yours.

—Harry S. Truman

We have always known that heedless self-interest was bad morals; we know now that it is bad economics.

—Benjamin Franklin

Economic systems are not value-free columns of numbers based on rules of reason, but ways of expressing what varying societies believe is important.

—Gloria Steinem
"Revaluing Economics," Moving Beyond Words, 1994

All economics is micro.

—Peggy Noonan
What I Saw at the Revolution: A Political Life in the Reagan Era, 1990

Fundamentally, there are only two ways of coordinating the economic activities of millions. One is central direction involving the use of coercion—the technique of the army and of the modern totalitarian state. The other is the voluntary cooperation of individuals—the technique of the market place.

—Milton Friedman
Capitalism and Freedom, 1962

The development of Modern Industry, therefore, cuts from under its feet the very foundation on which the bourgeoisie produces and appropriates products. What the bourgeoisie, therefore, produces, above all, are its own grave-diggers. Its fall and the victory of the proletariat are equally inevitable.

—K. Marx and F. Engels
The Communist Manifesto, 1848

East and West

East and West | Eastern

Culturally, there are many "Easts" and many "Wests" and they are by no means all necessarily irreconcilable.

—Peng Chun Chang
China at the Crossroads: The Chinese Situation in Perspective

I would heartily welcome the union of East and West provided it is not based on brute force.

—Mahatma Gandhi

All of us, East and West, are moving toward a new type of civilization whether we realize it or not. And it is that which compels me to think that our old stereotypes have now lost their meaning and should be radically re-examined.

—Mikhail S. Gorbachev
"No Time for Stereotypes," New York Times, February 24, 1992

We must recognize that it is providential that the West has come to India. And yet some one must show the East to the West, and convince the West that the East has her contribution to make to the history of civilization.

—Rabindranath Tagore
1925 speech, The World's Great Speeches

In the West, intellect is the source of life,
In the East, love is the basis of life.
Through love, intellect grows acquainted with reality,
And intellect gives stability to the work of love,
Arise and lay the foundations of a new world,
By wedding intellect to love.

—Iqbal
Reconstruction of Religious Thought in Islam

Asked about the distance between East and West, he replied: "One day's traveling for the sun."

—Ali

We may have torn down the walls between East and West, but we have yet to build the bridges between North and South—the rich and the poor.

—Mohamed ElBaradei
Nobel lecture, 2005

The answer to the North-South conflict, which is more serious than the East-West conflict, has to be found honestly and with unimpeachable integrity. Genuine disarmament will not come on its own or by platitudes at special sessions of the United Nations on disarmament, although, I was among the first to propose such a conference eighteen years ago.

—Zulfikar Ali Bhutto
Letter to his daughter (Benazir Bhutto), June 21, 1978

East and West | Western

But since there is only one earth and one mankind, East and West cannot rend humanity into two different halves.

—Carl Gustav Jung
Modern Man in Search of a Soul, 1933, trans. W. S. Bell and C. F. Payne

Oh, East is East, and West is West, and never the twain shall meet.
Till Earth and Sky stand presently at God's great Judgment Seat;
But there is neither East nor West, Border, nor Breed, nor Birth,
When two strong men stand face to face, though they come from the ends of the earth!

—Rudyard Kipling
The Ballad of East and West, 1892 poem

I do believe that there will be a clash between East and West. I believe that there will be a clash between those who want freedom, justice and equality for everyone and those who want to continue the systems of exploitation. I believe that there will be that kind of clash, but I don't think that it will be based upon the color of the skin.

—Malcolm X (El-Hajj Malik El-Shabazz)

Clearly, no longer can a dictator count on East-West confrontation...
Out of these troubled times, our fifth objective—a new world order... An era in which the nations of the world, east and west, north and south, can prosper and live in harmony.

—George Herbert Walker Bush

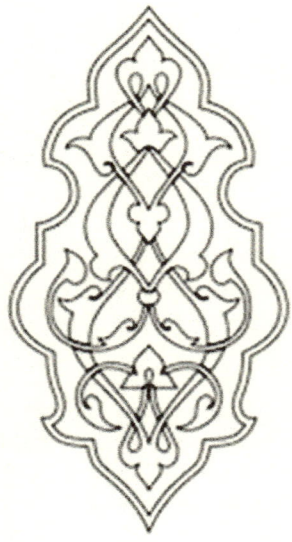

Education

Education | Eastern

One who believes all of a book would be better off without it.

—Mencius

When the student is ready, the master appears.

—Chinese proverb

He who learns and makes no use of his learning, is a beast of burden with a load of books [on its back].

—Sa'di

Education is a continuing process from the minute we are born until we die.

—Indira Gandhi

The treasure of learning is imperishable.

—Swami Dayanand

If you are planning for a year, plant grains;
If you are planning for a decade, plant trees;
If you are planning for a millennium, plant men.

—Chinese proverb

Every system of education basically consists of a set of certain societal ideals, norms and values and is based on a specific view of life and culture. It is in this realm that [absolute] imitation is suicidal. On the other hand as far as techniques and methods are concerned, one country can safely profit from the experiences of others.

—Khurshid Ahmad
Principles of Islamic Education

Education must not only seek to fill the young mind with knowledge, but must, at the same time, stimulate the child's moral character and stimulate him to the properties of social life.

—Al-Ghazali

The first and foremost task of the National Government is the provision of free and compulsory basic education for all.

—Abul Kalam Azad
Selected Works of Maulana Abul Kalam Azad

Education is the great engine of personal development. It is through education that the daughter of a peasant can become a doctor, that the son of a mineworker can become the head of the mine, that a child of farmworkers can become the president of a great nation. It is what we make out of what we have, not what we are given, that separates one person from another.

—Nelson Mandela
Long Walk to Freedom

This education has reduced us to a nation of morons; we were strangers to our own culture and camp followers of another culture, feeding on leavings and garbage... What about our own roots?... I am up against the system, the whole method and approach of a system of education which makes us morons, cultural morons, but efficient clerks for all your business and administration offices.

—R. K. Narayan
The English Teacher

Education | Western

How is it that little children are so intelligent and men so stupid? It must be the education that does it.

—Alexandre Dumas
In L. Treich, l'Esprit Francais, 1947

Not art, not books, but life itself is the true basis of... education.

—Johann H. Pestalozzi
The Education of Man: Aphorisms, trans. Heinz and Ruth Norden

Men of America, the problem is plain before you. Here is a race transplanted through the criminal foolishness of your fathers. Whether you like it or not the millions are here, and here they will remain. If you do not lift them up, they will pull you down. Education and work are the levers to uplift a people. Work alone will not do it unless inspired by the right ideals and guided by intelligence. Education must not simply teach work—it must teach life. The Talented Tenth of the Negro race must be made leaders of thought and missionaries of culture among their people. No others can do this and Negro colleges must train men for it. The Negro race, like all other races, is going to be saved by its exceptional men.

—W. E. B. Du Bois
"The Talented Tenth," The Negro Problem:
A Series of Articles by Representative Negroes of Today, 1903

Education is the art or process of imparting or acquiring knowledge and habits through instruction or study.

—John Dewey
Park, Dr. Joe, "Introduction," Selected Readings in the Philosophy of Education, 1958

The end of education is not "happiness" but rather to develop greater capacity for being aware; to deepen human understanding—perhaps inevitably through conflict; struggle and suffering—to make right action natural.

—W. R. Niblett
Education and the Modern Mind

Since education is a social process and there are many kinds of societies, a criterion for educational criticism and construction implies a particular social ideal.

—John Dewey

It (education) is a continuation of the process of growing into a full human being which took place physically in the nine months before we were born. But now it is the culture of the society which is the womb, and the spirit not the body which is gestated.

—W. R. Niblett

We must endeavor to teach even the unintelligent.

—Rashi (Rabbi Shlomo Itzhaki)

I do not believe that educational practices are an exportable commodity.

—Dr. J. B. Conant
Education and Liberty, 1953

If you think education is expensive, try ignorance!

—Derek Bok

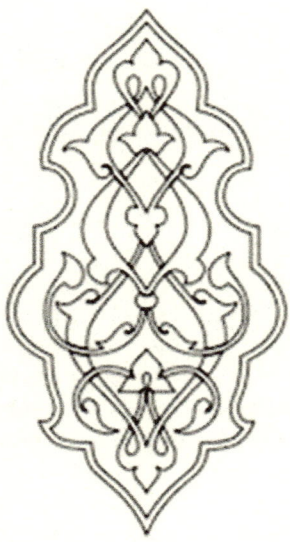

Ethics

Ethics | Eastern

Pride yourself on what virtue thou hast, and not on thy parentage.

—Sa'di

In doing good avoid fame. In doing bad, avoid disgrace. Pursue a middle course as your principle.

—Chuang Tzu

To the good I would be good; to the not-good I would also be good, in order to make them good.

—Lao Tzu
Tao Te Ching

It is enough for improving yourself that you should avoid what you consider bad in others.

—Ali
Nahj al-Balagha (Peak of Eloquence)

I have spent all my life under a communist regime and I will tell you that a society without any objective legal scale is a terrible one indeed. But a society with no other scale but the legal one is not quite worthy of man either. A society which is based on the letter of the law and never reaches any higher is taking very scarce advantage of the high level of human possibilities. The letter of the law is too cold and formal to have a beneficial influence on society.

—Aleksandr Solzhenitsyn

Every human being has two inclinations—one prompting him to good... and the other prompting him to evil...; but Divine assistance is near.

—Muhammad
Quoted in Al-Suhrawardy, The Sayings of Muhammad

There is enough light for one who wants to see.

—Ali

He who has no idea of evil can easily fall into its trap.

—Umar

If he does not know what is good, a man cannot be true to himself.

—Confucius

What has happened to us? It seems as if we have perverted our freedom, our rights into license, into being irresponsible. Perhaps we did not realize just how apartheid has damaged us so that we seem to have lost our sense of right and wrong.

—Desmond M. Tutu

Even if it is the king himself whom you find doing something improper, do not hesitate to call his attention to it.

—Abu Hanifa

If you remain quiet, and I remain quiet, how will the laymen know the right from wrong?

—Ibn Hanbal

Cut away evil from the chest of others by snatching (it) away from your own chest.

—Ali

Ethics | Western

In spite of everything I still believe that people are really good at heart.

—Anne Frank

Whoever fights with monsters should see to it that he does not become one himself. And when you stare for a long time into an abyss, the abyss stares back into you.

—Fredrick Nietzsche

No moral system can rest solely on authority.

—A. J. Ayer

The question for me is not what a lawyer tells me I may do, but what humanity, reason and justice tell me I ought to do.

—Edmund Burke

Sow a thought, and you reap an act;
Sow an act, and you reap a habit;
Sow a habit, and you reap a character;
Sow a character, and you reap a destiny.

—Charles Reade

Moderation in temper is always a virtue, moderation in principle is always a vice.

—Tom Paine

God considered not action, but the spirit of the action.

—Peter Abelard

While an ethic of justice proceeds from the premise of equality—that everyone should be treated the same—an ethic of care rests on the premise of nonviolence— that no one should be hurt.

—Carol Gilligan

Evil is unspectacular and always human,
And shares our bed and eats at our own table.

—W. H. Auden

There are two ways of spreading light: to be the candle or to be the mirror that refl ects it.

—Edith Wharton

The only thing necessary for the triumph of evil is for good men to do nothing.

—Edmund Burke

In matters of principle, stand like a rock.

—Thomas Jefferson

What lies behind us and what lies ahead of us are tiny matters compared to what lives within us.

—Ralph Waldo Emerson

Wrong is wrong no matter who says it.

—Malcolm X (El-Hajj Malik El-Shabazz)

Good and bad men are each less so than they seem.

—Samuel Taylor Coleridge
Table Talk

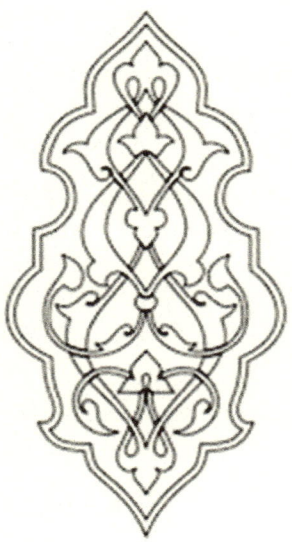

Existence

Existence | Eastern

To speak is to exist, to be heard and seen is to know that you exist.

—Anonymous

Existence is not by itself. Existence is by recognition.

—Krishnan Chander

Existence is the mother of all things.
From eternal non-existence, therefore, we serenely observe the mysterious beginning of the Universe; from eternal existence we clearly see the apparent distinctions.
These two are the same in source and become different when manifested

—Lao Tzu
Tao Te Ching

[E]xistence is the cause and reason of our knowledge, while eternal knowledge is the cause and reason of existence.

—Averroes (Ibn Rushd)
*The Book of the Decisive Treatise, Determining the Connection Between the
Law and Wisdom & Epistle Dedicatory, trans. Charles E. Butterworth*

Only [thing] that truly exists [is that] which can say "I am." It is the degree of the intuition of I-am-ness that determines the place of a thing in the scale of being.

—Iqbal
Reconstruction of Religious Thought in Islam

Existence | Western

Dubito ergo cogito, cogito ergo sum
I doubt therefore I think, I think therefore I exist.

—Rene Descartes

To speak is to exist

—Frantz Fanon

Credo ut intelligam
I believe, so that I may understand

—Anselm of Canterbury

Existence precedes essence.

—Jean-Paul Sartre
L'Existentialisme est un Humanisme, 1946

I don't know Who—or what—put the question,
I don't know when it was put. I don't even remember answering. But at some
moment I did answer yes to someone—or something—and from that hour
I was certain that existence is meaningful and that, therefore, my life, in self-
surrender, had a goal.

—Dag Hammarskjold
Markings, 1964

But I had persuaded myself that there was nothing at all in the world: no sky,
no earth, no minds or bodies: was I not also persuaded that I did not exist?
No indeed; I existed without doubt, by the fact that I thought at all.

—Rene Descartes
Discourse on Method and the Meditations, trans. F. E. Sutcliffe

False Hope and Despair

False Hope and Despair | Eastern

A man lost his way in the desert, and wandered aimlessly for several days. He ran out of food, and thought he would die. Then he saw a bag lying in the sand. He opened it, and at first he thought it was filled with grains of barley. He was overjoyed. But when he tried to eat them, he discovered they were pearls and he plunged into despair.

—Sa'di
The Gulistan (Rose Garden)

The entire world shall be populous with that action
of thine which saves one soul from despair.

—Omar Khayyam
Quoted in Pebbles, Pearls and Gems of the Orient, no. 52, 1882

This trembling light, this night-bitten dawn,
This is not the dawn, we have waited for so long
This is not the dawn whose birth was sired
By so many lives, so much blood
Generations ago, we started our confident march
Our hopes were young, our goals within reach
After all, there must be some limit
To the confusing constellation of stars
In a vast forest of the sky
Even the lazy languid waves
Must reach at last their appointed shore
And so we wistfully prayed
For a consummate end to our painful search
Many a temptation crossed our forbidden path
Many inviting bodies, many longing arms
Many seductive pleasures beckoned on our way
But we stayed faithful to our distant dream
We kept marching to a different drum
We kept searching for our lost freedom
We kept looking for our elusive dawn
We are told: our new dawn is already here;
Your tired feet need journey no more
Our rulers whisper seductively
Why this constant struggle? Why, this perpetual search
Come, join us, enjoy this new-found wealth

Built by the toil of our "liberated" poor
And yet, even today
Our hearts are aflame
Our desires unquenched
Our goals unmet
Was there a streak of light?
Where did it go?
The wayside lamp just blinked unawares
This is yet no relief in the darkness of the night
No liberation yet of our souls and minds
So let us keep marching, my tiring friends
We have yet to find our elusive dawn

—Faiz Ahmed Faiz

The Dawn of Freedom, trans. Mahbul Haq. Written in reference to the largely
unrealized hopes after Pakistan's independence from British occupation

False Hope and Despair | Western

Do not turn away, through cowardice, through despair. Go through it... pass beyond. On the other side of the tunnel you will find light again.

—Andre Gide

Despair is a greater sin than any of the sins which provoke it.

—C. S. Lewis

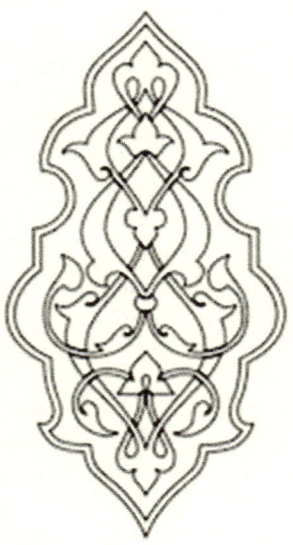

Fate

Fate | Eastern

No snowflake ever falls in the wrong place.

—Chinese proverb

It is a dark path—do not tread upon it, it is a deep ocean—do not dive in it, and it is the secret of Allah (God)—do not take trouble about it.

—Ali

Blind we stand before our fate,
Not ours to tear the veil from it.

—F. Tyutchev
Poems & Political Letters of F. I. Tyutchev, trans. Jesse Zeldin

If fate does not adjust to you, then you must adjust to it.

—Persian proverb

Let the days bring what they may,
and be content when a decree has come to pass,
when the execution of it comes in a land of some nation,
neither earth nor sky can prevent it.

—Al-Shafi 'i
Attributed

If you look only with the eye of predestination, you may miss a lot. You can't sit back and say, "We'll just go to sleep and wait to see what God will command."

—Shams of Tabriz
Rumi's Sun: The Teachings of Shams of Tabriz, 2008

Fate | Western

Must it be? It must be.

—Beethoven

Our ship of fate, which recent storms have threatened to destroy, has come safely to harbor at last.

—Sophocles

Cassius: The fault, dear Brutus, is not in our stars,
But in ourselves, that we are underlings.

—Shakespeare
Julius Caesar

I gather heart to risk the world's encounter,
To bear my human fate as fate's surmounter.

—Goethe
Faust, 1

Fools and Foolishness

Fools and Foolishness | Eastern

Baka wa shinanakya naoranai.
Only death will cure a fool.

—Japanese proverb

God has given me the power to give life to the dead, sight to the blind, sound to the deaf; but He did not give me the power to heal the fool of his foolishness.

—Jesus, Son of Mary
Cited by Al-Razi; Walk on Water:
The Wisdom of Jesus From traditional Arabic Sources, trans. Hamza Yusuf

Only a fool tests the depth of the water with both feet.

—African proverb

The fool is a cock which sings at the wrong time.

—Turkish proverb

O' My son, you should avoid making friends with a fool because he may intend to benefit you but may harm you.

—Ali

He desires to hide his tracks, and walks on snow.

—Chinese proverb

3alem fi e El-metbalem yesbahh nassi
Whatever you teach a fool, he will forget.

—Arabic proverb

As a dog returneth to his vomit, so a fool returneth to his folly.

—Proverb 26:11

The wise man never heard a joke
But living wisdom from it broke;
The fool no wisdom ever learned
But it in him to folly turned.

—Sa'di

Quoted in Pebbles, Pearls and Gems of the Orient

Fools and Foolishness | Western

Let us be thankful for the fools. But for them the rest of us could not succeed.
—Mark Twain (Samuel L. Clemens)

They never open their mouths without subtracting from the sum of human knowledge.
—Thomas B. Reed

There are no fools so troublesome as those that have wit.
—Benjamin Franklin

Self-satisfaction is the opiate of fools.

—Abraham Joshua Heschel
Who Is Man? 1965

It is hard to free fools from chains they revere.

—Voltaire

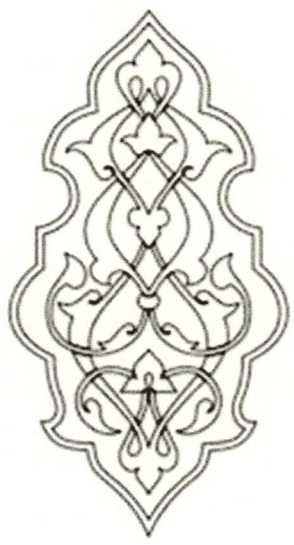

Freedom

Freedom | Eastern

The tree is not grateful to the dark house of dust—
In every moment the seed has the desire of growing.

—Iqbal
Zarb-i-Kali (Rod of Moses)

The sun shall never set on so glorious a human achievement!
God bless Africa!

—Nelson Mandela
Inaugural Celebration Address, May 10, 1994

When were you given Authority to deprive people of their freedom, when their mothers bore them as a free people!

—Umar

Freedom is the illusion of an imprisoned mind.

—Leonid S. Sukhorukov
All about Everything, 2005

Our freedom is but a light that breaks through from another world.

—Nikolai Gumilev
The Tram That Lost Its Way, 1921, trans. Dmitri Obolensky

Freedom demands respect for the freedom of others.

—Jawaharlal Nehru
Independence and After: A Collection of Speeches, 1946-1949

What freedom am I being offered while the organisation of the people remains banned? Only free men can negotiate. A prisoner cannot enter into contracts.

—Nelson Mandela
Allister Sparks, Tomorrow Is Another Country, 1994.

Conquerors always call themselves liberators.

—Sami Abdul-Rahman
Attributed

I have walked that long road to freedom. I have tried not to falter; I have made missteps along the way. But I have discovered the secret that after climbing a great hill, one only finds that there are many more hills to climb. I have taken a moment here to rest, to steal a view of the glorious vista that surrounds me, to look back on the distance I have come. But I can rest only for a moment, for with freedom comes responsibilities, and I dare not linger, for my long walk is not yet ended.

—Nelson Mandela
Long Walk to Freedom

Freedom | Western

Those who do not move, do not notice their chains

—Rosa Luxemburg

My dominion ends where that of conscience begins.

—Napoleon Bonaparte
In Ainsworth Rand Spofford, The Higher Law Tried by Reason and Authority, 1851

When a stone is rolling downhill it is free if there is nothing in its path.

—Thomas Hobbes

Authentic freedom is an outstanding manifestation of the divine image within man.

—Pope Paul VI
Gaudium et Spesn (Joy and Hope)

Freedom is participation in power.

—Marcus T. Cicero
Meditations

You can't separate peace from freedom because no one can be at peace unless he has his freedom.

—Malcolm X
Malcolm X Speaks, 1965

None can love freedom heartily but good men; the rest love not freedom, but license.

—John Milton

Debt is the slavery of the free.

—Syrus

If we don't believe in freedom of expression for people we despise, we don't believe in it at all.

—Noam Chomsky

No power on earth has a right to stand between God and the conscience.

—Philip Schaff
Church and State in the United States, 1888

Congress shall make no law... abridging the freedom of speech.

—Bill of Rights: First Amendment

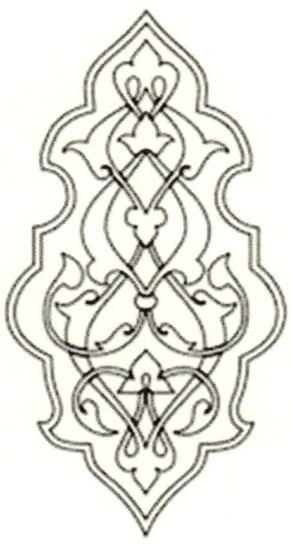

Friendship

Friendship | Eastern

To be chained by the feet with friends is better than to be free to walk in a garden with strangers.

—Sa'di

Friendship is always a sweet responsibility, never an opportunity.

—Kahlil Gibran

A friend is not a friend unless he affords protection to his comrade on three occasions: in his adversity, in his absence and at his death.

—Ali

Nahj al-Balagha (Peak of Eloquence)

Give up bad company.

—Abu Bakr
In Ghulam Sarwar, Islam Beliefs and Teaching

Do not be misled by someone's reputation.

—Umar
In Ghulam Sarwar, Islam Beliefs and Teachings

He who was my friend knew me not and went away...
He saw my outer being but not the inner one.

—Iqbal
Mohammed Iqbal, Poet and Philosopher

Better a wise enemy than a foolish friend.

—Arabic proverb

A sudden thought strikes me; let us swear an eternal friendship.

—John Hookham Frer

Two may talk together under the same room for many years, yet never really meet; and two others at fi rst speech are old friends.

—Mary Catherwood

It is easier to guard against an enemy than against a friend.

—Alcamaeon

There will be not only peace between us and the Arabs,... but close friendship and co-operation.

—Ben Gurion,
To Anglo-American Com. of Inquiry in March 19, 1946

No guest is so welcome in a friend's house that he will not become a nuisance after three days.

—Plautus

He that is thy friend indeed. He will help thee in thy need.

—Shakespeare

'Tis great Confidence in a Friend to tell your Faults, greater to tell him his.

—Benjamin Franklin

What is yours is mine, and all that is mine is yours.

—Plautus

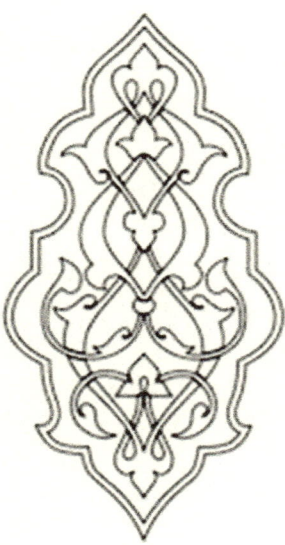

Future

Future | Eastern

Without forgiveness, there's no future.

—Archbishop Desmond Tutu

Who heeds not the future, will fi nd sorrow at hand.

—Confucius

There was the door to which I found no key;
There was the veil through which I might not see.

—Omar Khayyam
Quoted in The Rubaiyat of Omar Khayyam, trans. Fitzgerald

Time's wheel runs back or stops: potter and clay endure.

—Rabbi Ben Ezra

Do not defer your work for tomorrow.

—Umar
In Ghulam Sarwar, Islam Beliefs and Teachings

One day our grandchildren will go to museums to see what poverty was like.
—Muhammad Yunus
Australian Broadcasting Corporation, March 25, 1997

Future | Western

Due to a lack of interest, tomorrow has been canceled.

—Irene Kampen
Due to Lack of Interest, Tomorrow Has Been Canceled, 1969

The future must be shaped or it will impose itself as a catastrophe.

—Henry A. Kissinger
Years of Upheaval, 1982

The empires of the future are the empires of the mind.

—Winston Churchill

Lord! We know what we are but we know not what we may be.

—Shakespeare

I shrink from words evoking future ruin.

—Gaius Petronius

The future is purchased by the present.

—Samuel Johnson

Not enjoyment, and not sorrow,
Is our destined end or way;
But to act, that each to-morrow
Find us farther than to-day.

—Henry W. Longfellow
Psalm of Life

Generosity

Generosity | Eastern

It is more blessed to give than to receive.

—Acts 20:35

You give but little when you give of your possessions. It is when you give of yourself that you truly give.

—Kahlil Gibran

Let your hand not be stretched out to take, and closed at the time of giving back.

—Ben Sira

If you have much give of your wealth, if you have little give of your heart.

—Arabic proverb

Forget not generosity among yourselves.

—Qur'an 2:237

'En kan habibak 3asal ma-telhasoush kolloh
If your friend is like honey, then don't lick all of them!
[Do not take advantage of a friend's generosity.]

—Egyptian proverb

Generosity | Western

It is in giving that we receive.

—St. Francis of Assisi

Give all thou canst; high Heaven rejects
The lore
Of nicely-calculated less or more.

—William Wordsworth

People who think they're generous to a fault usually think that's their only fault.
—Sydney J. Harris
On the Contrary, 1962

Give soon and you give twice.

—Publilius Syrus

The good man thinks it more blessed to give than to receive.

—Aristotle

Nicomachean Ethics, 4.1, trans. J. A. K. Thomson, 1953

He that gives quickly gives twice.

—Cervantes

Don Quixote, trans. Peter Anthony Motteux and John Ozell, 1743

Put justice before generosity.

—Irish proverb

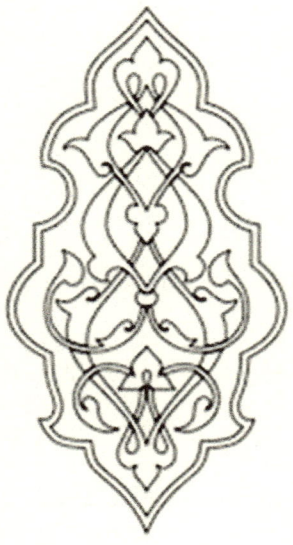

Great People

Great People | Eastern

The principles of great men illuminate the universe.

—Mencius
Quoted in Pebbles, Pearls and Gems of the Orient, no. 50, 1882

Our soul discovers itself when we come into contact with a great mind.

—Iqbal
Thoughts and reflections of Iqbal

The lights of stars that were extinguished ages ago still reaches us. So it is with great men who died centuries ago, but still reach us with the radiations of their personalities.

—Kahlil Gibran

I am a leader by default, only because nature does not allow a vacuum.

—Desmond M. Tutu
As quoted in The Christian Science Monitor, 20 December 1984

The best of men is he who strikes what is right without effort.

—Confucius

In this world I would rather live two days like a tiger, than two hundred years like a sheep.

—Tipu Sultan

How shall we praise him and how shall we measure him, because he was not of the common clay that all of us are made of?... A glory has departed and the sun that warmed and brightened our lives has set and we shiver in the cold and dark.

—Jawaharlal Nehru
Speech given in front of Constitutional Assembly on
2 Feb. 1948 after the passing of Gandhi. The World's Great Speeches

Never has there been one possessed of complete sincerity who did not move others.

—Mencius

Grieve not that men know you not; grieve that you know not men.

—Confucius

Great People | Western

If I have seen further it is by standing on the shoulders of giants.

—Sir Isaac Newton

When we come to the study of great men it is easy to think only of their great deeds, and not to think enough of their spirit. What is a great man who has made his mark upon history? Every time, if we think far enough, he is a man who has looked through the confusion of the moment and has seen the moral issue involved; he is a man who has refused to have his sense of justice distorted; he has listened to his conscience until conscience becomes a trumpet call to like-minded men, so that they gather about him and together, with mutual purpose and mutual aid.

—Jane Addams
In an Address at the Union League Club on Washington's Birthday, 1904

Lives of great men all remind us.
We can make our lives sublime,
And, departing, leave behind us.
Footprints on the sands of time.

—Henry W. Longfellow

Andrea: Unhappy the land that has no heroes!
Galileo: No, unhappy the land that needs heroes.

—Bertold Brecht

My Sin City heroes are knights in dirty, blood-caked armor. They bring justice to a world that gives them no medals, no praise, no reward. That world, that city, often kills them for their brave service.

—Frank Miller
"Frank Miller: I Stole from the Best!" COMICDOM interview, January 22, 2006

The really great man is the man who makes every man feels great.

—G. K. Chesterton

How important it is for us to recognize and celebrate our heroes and she-roes!

—Maya Angelou
In Chris Orr, "Moms and Whoopi: Pioneers of Black Theater," Plexus, November 1983

Show me a hero, and I will write you a tragedy.

—F. Scott Fitzgerald
"The Note-books," The Crack-up

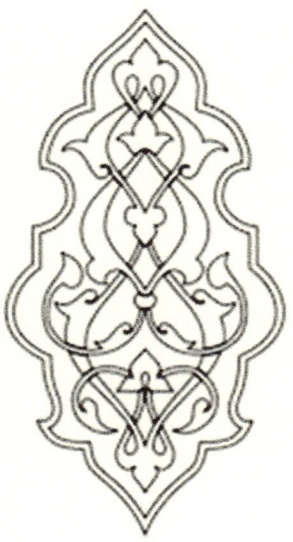

Happiness

Happiness | Eastern

Keep a green tree in your heart and perhaps a songbird will come.
—Chinese proverb

The drop grows happy by losing itself in the river.
—Mirza Ghalib
Attributed

Every night is the grand night provided you appreciate its worth.
—Persian proverb

Happiness depends on what you can give, not what you can get.
—Mahatma Gandhi

With coarse rise to eat, with water to drink, and my bended arm for a pillow, I have still joy in the midst of these things. Riches and honors acquired by unrighteousness are to me as a floating cloud.
—Confucius

We choose our joys and sorrows long before we experience them.
—Kahlil Gibran

Contentment and gratitude are two great virtues; you should not care which one you are gaining.
—Umar
In Ghulam Sarwar, Islam Beliefs and Teachings

My greatest happiness consists precisely doing nothing whatever calculated to obtain happiness.
—Chuang-Tzu

Pronounce no man happy before his death, for by his latter end shall a man be known.
—Ben Sira

All happy families resemble one another; each unhappy family is unhappy in its own way.
—Leo Tolstoy

Ignore pain otherwise you will never be happy.

—Ali

[It is] the message of death to remain in the negation.

—Iqbal
Zarb-i-Kalim

Happy is the one who gives his eye and his heart.
What a shame that they give their eyes
but not their hearts.
Happy is the one whose eyes sleep,
but whose heart doesn't sleep!
Woe to the one whose eyes do not sleep
but whose heart does!

—Shams of Tabriz
Rumi's Sun: The Teachings of Shams of Tabriz, 2008

Happiness | Western

Oh! how bitter a thing it is to look into happiness through another man's eyes.
—Shakespeare
As You Like It

Those who are happiest are those who do the most for others.
—Booker T. Washington
Up from Slavery: An Autobiography, 1901

What ultimately moves our desires?
Happiness, and that alone. It is the utmost pleasure of which men are due.
—John Locke

Glad that I Live am I;
That the sky is blue;
Glad for the country lanes,
And the fall of dew.

—Lizette W. Reese
A Little Song of Life

The summit of happiness is reached when a person is ready to be what he is.
—Erasmus

Happiness is no laughing matter.
—Richard Whately

Happiness is not an ideal of reason but of imagination.
—Immanuel Kant

Many persons have a wrong idea of what constitutes true happiness. It is not attained through self-gratification but through fidelity to a worthy purpose.
—Helen Keller
Helen Keller's Journal

The greatest griefs are those we cause ourselves.
—Sophocles

Oedipus Rex

Happy people are constantly evaluating themselves and unhappy people are constantly evaluating others.
—William Glasser

Under all skies, all weathers, man's happiness lies always elsewhere; sorrow lives and reigns.
—Giacomo Leopardi

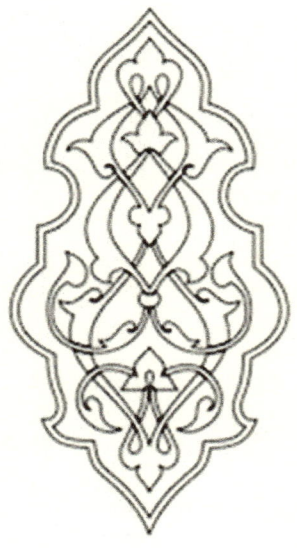

Heart

Heart | Eastern

What was said to the rose that made it open was said to me here in my chest.

—Rumi

God desires the heart.

—The Talmud

A good head and a good heart are always a formidable combination.

—Nelson Mandela
Long Walk to Freedom

The heart is the book of the eye.

—Ali

For in one soul are contained the hopes and feelings of all mankind.

—Kahlil Gibran
The Voice of the Master

Son, if you are able, keep your heart free from malice.

—Muhammad

Our hearts burn but no clouds of smoke pour out.

—Mirza Ghalib
Quoted in Natalia Prigarina, Mirza Ghalib: A Creative Biography

The moth that flew to the candle was lost:
it went after the light and fell into the fire.

—Shams of Tabriz
Rumi's Sun: The Teachings of Shams of Tabriz, 2008

Heart | Western

The heart has its reasons, which reason does not know.

—Blaise Pascal

Calm of mind, all passion spent.

—John Milton

The human heart is vast enough to contain all the world.

—Joseph Conrad
Lord Jim, 1900

Speak to his heart, and the man becomes suddenly virtuous.

—Ralph Waldo Emerson
Journal, October 11, 1839

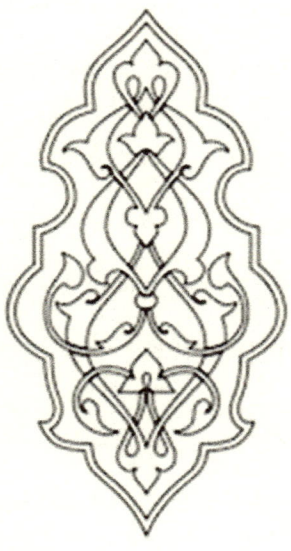

History

History | Eastern

The moving finger writes; and, having writ,
Moves on: nor all thy piety nor wit
Shall lure it back to cancel half a line,
Nor all thy tears wash out a word of it.

—Omar Khayyam
Quoted in The Rubaiyat of Omar Khayyam, trans. Fitzgerald

When a word has once escaped, a chariot with four
horses cannot overtake it. Learn then to watch over
thy words.
—Chinese proverb The people, and the people alone, are the motive force in
the making of world history.

—Mao Tse-tung
"On Coalition Government," April 23, 1945, Selected Works of Mao Tse-tung

Whether you like it or not, history is on our side. We will bury you.

—Nikita Khrushchev
Speech to Western diplomats at Polish embassy, November 18, 1956

The inner meaning of history... involves speculation and an attempt to get
at the truth.

—Ibn Khaldun
The Muqaddimah: An Introduction to History

History, like beauty, depends largely on the beholder, so when you read that,
for example, David Livingstone discovered the Victoria Falls, you might be
forgiven for thinking that there was nobody around the falls until Livingstone
arrived on the scene.

—Desmond M. Tutu

History shows that there are no invincible armies.

—Joseph Stalin

[History] requires numerous sources and various knowledge.

—Ibn Khaldun
The Muqaddimah: An Introduction to History

We stand at the end of an era and on the threshold of a new period of history. Standing on this watershed which divides two epochs of human history and endeavour, we can look back on our long past and look forward to the future that is taking shape before our eyes.

—Jawaharlal Nehru
1947 speech. The World's Great Speeches

The world is full of stories of folk gone by, but unless one lends an ear to it, its call is weak.

—Persian Couplet

illei faat maat
What is past is dead.

—Egyptian proverb

We, in India, must make up our minds that we cannot borrow other people's history, and that if we stifle our own we are committing suicide.

—Rabindranath Tagore
1925 speech, The World's Great Speeches

History | Western

Those who cannot learn from history are doomed to repeat it.

—George Santayana

History will bear me out, particularly as I shall write that history myself.

—Winston Churchill

"Who controls the past," ran the Party slogan, "controls the future: who controls the present controls the past."

—George Orwell

History is bunk.

—Henry Ford

What is history but a fable agreed upon?

—Napoleon Bonaparte

As a professor, I tended to think of history as run by impersonal forces. But when you see it in practice, you see the differences personalities make.

—Henry Kissinger
Introduction (epigraph) to Kissinger: A Biography, 1992, by Walter Isaacson

[History] can both warn and inspire. It can warn us that it is possible for a whole nation to be brainwashed, for "enlightened" and "educated" people to commit genocide, for a "democratic" country to maintain slavery, for oppressed to turn into oppressors, for "socialism" to be tyrannical and "liberalism" to be imperialist, for whole peoples to be led to war like sheep. It can also show us that apparently powerless underlings can defeat their rulers, that men (for at least moments of time) can live like brothers, that man can make incredible sacrifices on behalf of a cause.

—Howard Zinn
The Politics of History, 1970

What we may be witnessing is not the end of the Cold War but the end of history as such; that is, the end point of man's ideological evolution and the universalization of Western liberal democracy.

—Francis Fukuyama
Writing of the impact of the end of the Cold War. In National Interest, Summer 1989

History is the record of what one age finds worthy of note in another.

—Jacob Burckhardt

Challenge-and-response resembles cause-and-effect only in standing for a sequence of events. The character of the sequence is not the same. Unlike the effect of a cause, the response to a challenge is not predetermined… and is therefore intrinsically unpredictable.

—Arnold Toynbee
A Study of History

History is written by the winners.

—George Orwell

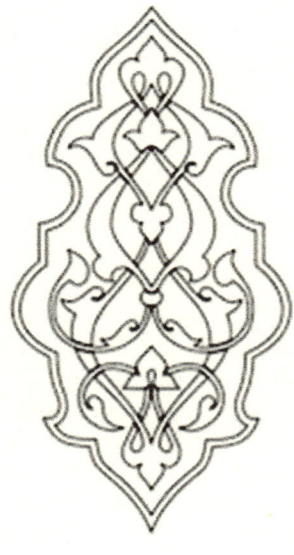

Hope

Hope | Eastern

Hope to the end.

—1 Peter

For the man who has eyes, the dawn has already appeared.

—Ali

South Africa, so utterly improbably, is a beacon of hope in a dark and troubled world.

—Desmond M. Tutu

Hope deferred makes the heart sick.

—Christian proverb

The dark blue sky is never empty of new stars.

—Iqbal

Zarb-i-Kalim

I have hope because the positive aspects of globalization are enabling nations and peoples to become politically, economically and socially interdependent, making war an increasingly unacceptable option... I have hope because civil society is becoming better informed and more engaged. They are pressing their governments for change—to create democratic societies based on diversity, tolerance and equality. They are proposing creative solutions. They are raising awareness, donating funds, working to transform civic spirit from the local to the global. Working to bring the human family closer together.

—Mohamed ElBaradei
Nobel lecture, 2005

Hope | Western

The work goes on, the cause endures, the hope still lives, and the dream shall never die.

—Ted Kennedy

Concession speech in his campaign for nomination as the Democratic Presidential candidate against incumbent Jimmy Carter at the Democratic Convention in New York City, August 12, 1980

Hope dies last.

—Mexican proverb

Take hope from the heart of man and you make him a beast of prey.
—Ouida (Marie Louise de la Ramee)

In all things it is better to hope than to despair.

—Goethe

No condition so low but many have Hopes, none so high but may have Fears.
—Thomas Fuller
Gnomologia: Adages and Proverbs, 3555, 1732

Hold your head high, stick your chest out. You can make it. It gets dark sometimes but morning comes... Keep hope alive!
—Rev. Jesse Jackson

Hope springs eternal in the human breast:
Man never is, but always to be blest.

—Alexander Pope
An Essay on Man, 1734

If it were not for hope the heart would break.

—John Ray
A Collection of English Proverbs, 1678

In the end, that's what this election is about. Do we participate in a politics of cynicism or a politics of hope? I'm not talking about blind optimism here... No, I'm talking about something more substantial. It's the hope of slaves sitting around a fire singing freedom songs;

the hope of immigrants setting out for distant shores; the hope of a young naval lieutenant bravely patrolling the Mekong Delta; the hope of a millworker's son who dares to defy the odds; the hope of a skinny kid with a funny name who believes that America has a place for him, too. The audacity of hope!

—President Barak Hussein Obama

Speech at the Democratic National Convention, July 27, 2004

Humanity

Humanity | Eastern

You must not lose faith in humanity.

—Gandhi
Gandhi: His Life and Message for the World, 1954

Tsze-Kung asked, saying, "Is there one word which may serve as a rule of practice for all one's life?" The Master said, "Is not Reciprocity such a word? What you do not want done to yourself, do not do to others."

—Confucius
The Analects

The global community has become irreversibly interdependent, with the constant movement of people, ideas, goods and resources.
If the world does not change course, we risk self-destruction.

—Mohamed ElBaradei
"Saving Ourselves From Self-Destruction," New York Times, February 12, 2004

Human beings are members of a whole,
In creation of one essence and soul.
If one member is afflicted with pain,
Other members uneasy will remain.
If you have no sympathy for human pain,
The name of human you cannot retain.

—Sa'di
The poem graces the UN building in New York. The Gulistan (Rose Garden), 1258

I understood that God does not wish men to live apart, and therefore he does not reveal to them what each one needs for himself; but he wishes them to live united, and therefore reveals to each of them what is necessary for all.

—Leo Tolstoy

I think the ultimate sense of security will be when we come to recognize that we are all part of one human race. Our primary allegiance is to the human race and not to one particular color or border. I think the sooner we renounce the sanctity of these many identities and try to identify ourselves with the human race the sooner we will get a better world and a safer world.

—Mohamed ElBaradei
"Breaking the Cycle," Cairo Times, October 23, 2003

Humanity | Western

E Pluribus Unum
Out of many, one.

—Seal of the United States

We declare our right on this earth to be a human being, to be respected as a human being, to be given the rights of a human being, in this society, on this earth, in this day, which we intend to bring into existence by any means necessary.

—Malcolm X
Speech at Founding Rally of the Organization of Afro-American Unity

Liberty is human rights.

—Jimmy Carter
Farewell Address, January 14, 1981

What shadows we are, and what shadows we pursue.

—Edmund Burke
Speech, Bristol (England), September 9, 1780

We are single cells in a body of three billion cells. The body is humankind.

—Norman Cousins
"Editor's Odyssey: Gleanings from Articles and Editorials by N. C.," Saturday Review,
April 15, 1978

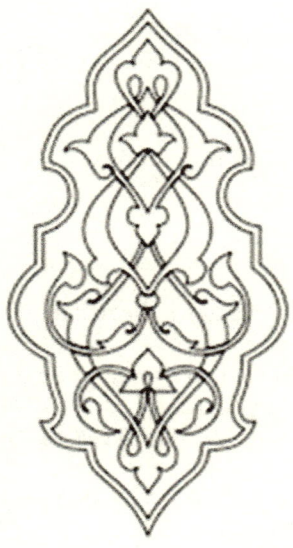

Ideas

Ideas | Eastern

Ideas are far more powerful than guns.

—Joseph Stalin

Everybody lives and acts partly according to other people's ideas.

—Leo Tolstoy

Timid thoughts, do not be afraid of me. I am the poet.

—Rabindranath Tagore

Life is preserved by purpose and idea;
Because of the goal its caravan bell tinkles.

—Iqbal

I don't adopt any one's ideas; I have my own.

—Ivan Turgenev
Fathers and Sons, 1862

Ideas | Western

But the idea of the nest in the bird's mind, where does it come from?
—Samuel Johnson
In James Boswell, The Life of Samuel Johnson, 1791

V: Beneath this mask there is more than flesh. Beneath this mask there is an idea. . . and ideas are bulletproof.

—V for Vendetta
By the Wachowski brothers, based on the comic series by Alan Moore

Gibraltar may be strong, but ideas are impregnable, and bestow on the hero their invincibility.

—Ralph Waldo Emerson
"The American Civilization," The Atlantic Monthly, 1862

Nothing is more common than for men to think that because they are familiar with words they understand the ideas they stand for.
—Cardinal John Newman

Evey Hammond: We are told to remember the idea, not the man, because a man can fail. He can be taught, he can be killed and forgotten but, 400 years later, an idea can still change the world. I've witnessed firsthand the power of ideas, I've seen people kill in the name of them, and die defending them... but you cannot kiss an idea, cannot touch it, or hold it... ideas do not bleed, they do not feel pain, they do not love.

—V for Vendetta
By the Wachowski brothers, based on the comic series by Alan Moore

Man's mind, stretched by a new idea, never goes back to its original dimensions.
—Oliver Wendell Holmes

A man may die, nations may rise and fall, but an idea lives on.
—John F. Kennedy

No army can withstand the strength of an idea whose time has come.
—Victor Hugo

Ideas shape the course of human history.

—John M. Keynes

Ideas come from God.

—Albert Einstein
Remark to the author. In Banesh Hoffman,
"My Friend, Albert Einstein," Reader's Digest, January 1968

There is nothing so powerful as an old idea whose time has come again.
—Ben Wattenberg
Quoted by Hugh Sidey, Washington Star, May 6, 1979

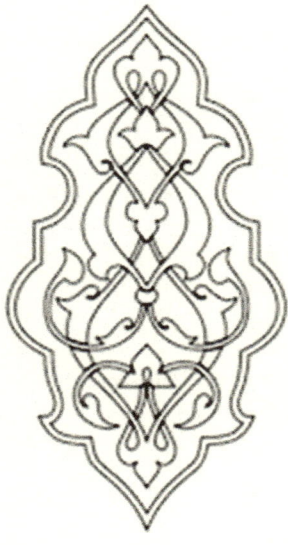

Imagination and Abstract Thinking

Imagination and Abstract Thinking | Eastern

There is no branch of mathematics, however abstract, which may not, some day, be applied to phenomena of the real world.

—Nikolai Ivanovich Lobachevsky

Imagination is a clear mirror, and the taking of lessons (from things around) provides warning and council.

—Ali
Nahj al-Balagha (Peak of Eloquence)

Don't give so much rein to your imagination—it does no good and only wastes your time.

—Rabindranath Tagore

Imagine what would happen if the nations of the world spent as much on development as on building the machines of war. Imagine a world where every human being would live in freedom and dignity... Imagine that such a world is within our grasp.

—Mohamed ElBaradei
Nobel lecture, 2005

The roses of imagination and craftsmanship is always at a loss [invaluable commodity].

—Anonymous Eastern poem

Imagination and Abstract Thinking | Western

What is now proved was once only imagin'd.

—William Blake
"Proverbs of Hell," The Marriage of Heaven and Hell, 1790-1793

Science does not know its debt to imagination.

—Ralph Waldo Emerson
Poetry and Imagination, 1872

To see a world in a grain of sand
And a heaven in a wild flower

Hold infinity in the palm of your hand
And eternity in an hour

—William Blake

The ability to climb to higher and higher levels of abstraction is a distinctively human trait, without which none of our philosophical or scientific insights would be possible. In order to have a science of chemistry, one has to be able to think of "H_2O,..." Thinking that is most abstract can also be that which is most generally useful... a brilliant generalization at so high a level of abstraction that it appears to be applicable to all men of all cultures.

—S. I. Hayakawa
Language in Thought and Action, 1964

Where jargon turns living issues into abstractions, and where jargon ends by competing with jargon, people don't have causes. They only have enemies.

—V. S. Naipul
Nobel lecture

The human race is governed by its imagination.

—Napoleon Bonaparte

He who has imagination without learning has wings and not feet.

—Joseph Joubert
Pensees, 1838, trans. Henry Attwell, 1877

The world of reality has its bounds, the world of imagination is boundless.

—Rousseau

Quoted in Treatise on Education, 1762, trans. Barbara Foxley, 1911

A spider conducts operations that resemble those of a weaver, and a bee puts to shame many an architect in the construction of her cells. But what distinguishes the worst architect from the best of bees is this, that the architect raises his structure in imagination before he erects it in reality.

—Karl Marx

Das Kapital: Kritik der politischen Ökonomie (Capital)

Innovation and Imitation

Innovation and Imitation | Eastern

The imitator will always remain a step behind the innovator.

—Agha K. Saeed

You cannot stop innovation.

—Sun Tzu
The Art of War

Look into thy own clay for the fire that is wanted
The light of another is not worth striving for.

—Iqbal
Payam-i-Mashriq (Message from the East)

How long will thou abide under the wings of others? Learn to wing thy flight freely in the garden breeze.

—Iqbal
Diwan-i-Iqbal

Now, since you are a human being, how can it be that you don't speak—that your tongue doesn't start talking—but you just keep repeating some old wives' tale or Arabic poems! That's it! Now, where are your own words?

—Shams of Tabriz
Rumi's Sun: The Teachings of Shams of Tabriz, 2008

Innovation and Imitation | Western

O imitators, you slavish herd!

—Horace
Epistles, 1.19

Imitate what is good wheresoever thou findest it.

—Thomas Fuller
Introductio ad Prudentiam, 1731

Genius... is the child of imitation.

—Sir Joshua Reynolds
Discourses on Art

We imitate only what we believe and admire.

—Willmot

Imitation is the sincerest (form) of flattery.

—C. C. Colton

Monkey see, monkey do.

—Anonymous

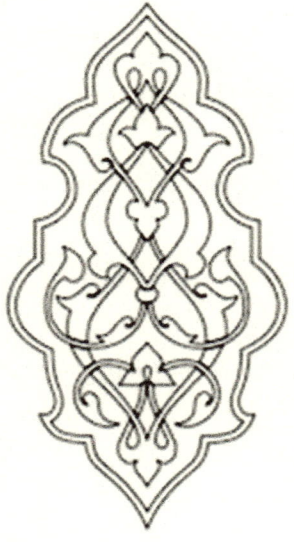

Intellect and Intellectual

Intellect and Intellectual | Eastern

Iron sharpens iron, scholar the scholar.

—Jewish proverb

The prosperity and advancement of a nation depend upon its intelligentsia.

—Jinnah
Comment made on December 24, 1940

No ruling class can endure without its intelligentsia.

—Joseph Stalin
In Eric Hoffer, The Ordeal of Change, 1964

Eyes are of little use if the mind is blind.

—Arabic proverb

No one will have perfect religion until he/she has perfect intellect.

—Hassan al-Basri

At forty, I had attained the unperturbed mind.

—Mencius

The ink of the scholar is more holy than the blood of the martyr.

—Muhammad

Intellect and Intellectual | Western

My mind to me a kingdom is.

—Sir Edward Dyer

1586 poem

And still they gaz'd, and still the
wonder grew,
That one small head could carry
All he knew.

—Oliver Goldsmith

When the intellectual comes into his own, he becomes a pillar of stability and
fi nds all kinds of lofty reasons for siding with the strong against the weak.

—Eric Hoffer
The Ordeal of Change, 1964

The intellectual whose capital is his knowledge.

—Harold D. Lasswell
Daniel Lerner and C. Easton Rothwell,
The Comparative Study of Elites: An Introduction and Bibliography, 1952

No one has ever devised a method for detaching the scholar from the circumstances
of life, from the fact of his involvement (conscious or unconscious) with a class,
a set of beliefs, a social position, or from the mere activity of being a member
of a society.

—Edward Said
Orientalism, 1978

Intelligence

Intelligence | Eastern

You can tell whether a man is clever by his answers. You can tell whether a man is wise by his questions.

—Naguib Mahfouz

He who exerts his mind to the utmost knows his nature.

—Mencius (Mèng Zǐ)
Mencius, Chan, 1963

Human intellect at birth is rather like a tabula rasa (empty slate), a pure potentiality that is actualized through education and comes to know.

—Avicenna (Ibn Sina)
H. Rizvi, Internet Encyclopedia of Philosophy, 2006

Judge a man's intelligence by the question he asks.

—Umar
In Ghulam Sarwar, Islam Beliefs and Teachings

Intelligence | Western

Great minds discuss ideas. Average minds discuss events. Small minds discuss people.

—Eleanor Roosevelt

The trouble with the world is that the stupid are cocksure and the intelligent full of doubt.

—Bertrand Russell

No problem can be solved from the same consciousness that created it. We must learn to see the world anew.

—Albert Einstein

There are men who can think no deeper than a fact.

—Voltaire
Quoted in Thesaurus of Epigrams, by Edmund Fuller

If an animal does something, we call it instinct; if we do the same thing for the same reason, we call it intelligence.

—Willy Cuppy

The third-rate mind is only happy when it is thinking with the majority. The second-rate mind is only happy when it is thinking with the minority. The first-rate mind is only happy when it is thinking.

—A. Milne

Jealousy and Anger

Jealousy and Anger | Eastern

Jealousy devours virtue as fire devours fuel.

—Ali
The Muslim 100: The Lives, Thoughts and Achievements of the Most Influential
Muslims in History

Anger deprives a sage of his wisdom.

—The Talmud

Indulge not thyself in the passion of Anger; it is whetting a sword to wound thine own breast, or murder thy friend.

—Akhenaton (Amenhotep IV)

When anger rises, think of the consequences.

—Confucius (K'ung-Fu-Tzu)
The Analects

There is no [good in] jealousy except with respect to two people: A person whom Allah (God) has given wealth and he uses it for the sake of the truth and a person whom Allah (God) has given wisdom and he decides by it and acts accordingly.

—Muhammad
Sahih al-Bukhari

Jealousy and Anger | Western

Captain Ahab to Moby-Dick: From hell's heart I stab at thee; for hate's sake I spit my last breath at thee.

—Herman Melville
Moby-Dick

V: The only verdict is vengeance; a vendetta held as a votive, not in vain, for the value and veracity of such shall one day vindicate the vigilant and the virtuous.

—Steve Moore
The Novelization of V for Vendetta, 2006

The proud man hath no God; the envious man hath no neighbor; the angry man hath not himself.

—Joseph Hall
Reported in Josiah Hotchkiss Gilbert, Dictionary of Burning Words of Brilliant Writers,
1895

Anger and jealousy can no more bear to lose sight of their objects than love.

—Mary Ann Evans (George Eliot)
The Mill on the Floss, book I, 1860

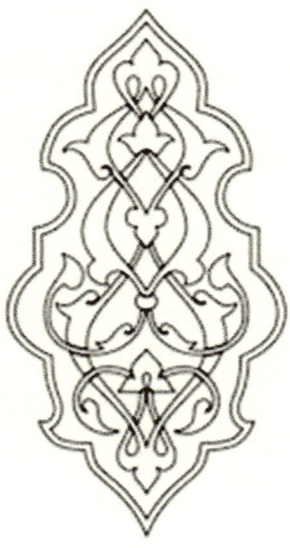

Judging

Judging | Eastern

Judge every man in the most favorable light.

—Hebrew proverb

Judge not, that you not be judged.

—Christian proverb

Think lightly of yourself and think deeply of the world.
—Miyamoto Musashi
Go Rin No Sho (The Book of Five Rings), 1645

Judge not your neighbor till you've been in his place.

—Hillel

You may judge a flower or a butterfly by its looks, but not a human being.
—Rabindranath Tagore

Be your own judge and you will be happy.

—Mahatma Gandhi

el-faDi ye3mel 'aDi
The idle are busy judging others.

—Egyptian proverb

Judging | Western

Be to her virtues very kind,
Be to her faults a little blind.

—Prior

When a man points a finger at someone else, he should remember that four of his fingers are pointing at himself.

—Louis Nizer

Men in general, judge more from appearances than from reality. All men have eyes, but few have the gift of penetration.

—Machiavelli

Men are not judged by their words... but by their actions.

—Fredrick II
Anti-Machiavel, 1740, trans. Paul Sonnino, 1981

The world is full of posts jeering at kettles.

—La Rochefoucauld
Maxims, 507, 1665, trans. Leonard Tancock, 1959

People who live in a glass houses shouldn't throw stones.

—English language proverb

Knowledge

Knowledge | Eastern

Every source is a pen.

—Al Kindhi
Attributed

He who esteems himself highly because of his <u>knowledge</u> is like a corpse at the wayside.

—Akiba Ben Joseph

Knowledge is the conformity of the object and the intellect.

—Averroes

Every container gets narrower according to what is placed in it except knowledge which expands instead.

—Ali
Nahj al-Balagha (Peak of Eloquence)

On the inference drawn by (blind) men touching different parts of the same elephant in the dark. In the end each of them arrive at different conclusions of what an elephant looks like; to the one who touches it's ear, elephants are flat, for the one touching its tail, elephants are long and skinny, and for the one touching its feet, they resemble the trunk of a tree.

—Rumi
Mathnawi

A little knowledge that acts is worth infinitely more than much knowledge that is idle.
—Kahlil Gibran

Knowledge raises the low, but ignorance brings down the mighty. —Ali
Knowledge is of two kinds: that which is absorbed and that which is heard. And that which is heard does not profit if it is not absorbed.

—Ali
Nahj al-Balagha (Peak of Eloquence)

Knowledge alone effects emancipation.
As fire is indispensable to cooking,
So knowledge is essential to deliverance.

—Shankara
Atma-Bodha

The master said, "Yu, shall I teach you what knowledge is? When you know a thing, to recognize that you know it, and when you do not know a thing, to recognize that you do not know it. That is knowledge."

—Confucius
The Analects

He who learns and makes no use of his learning, is a beast of burden with a load of books [on its back].

—Sa'di

Allah (God) loves the (faithful) scholar more than a thousand worshippers.

—Islamic proverb

Knowledge | Western

I want to know God's thoughts—the rest are mere details.

—Albert Einstein
Quoted in "Einstein's Unfinished Symphony," BBC Science & Nature

Knowledge which is applicable to no useful purpose, cannot deserve the name of wisdom.

—Ennius

There is no darkness but ignorance.

—Shakespeare

Knowledge is power.

—Francis Bacon
Meditationes Sacræ (Sacred Meditations), 1597

A little learning is a dangerous thing.

—Alexander Pope
Essay on Criticism

Never learn to do anything: if you don' learn, you'll always find someone else to do it for you.

—Mark Twain

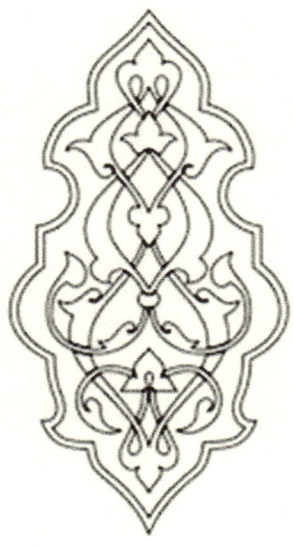

Language

Language | Eastern

Language influences the way in which we perceive reality.

—Peter Mwaura

The tongue is but three inches long yet it can kill a man six feet high.

—Japanese proverb

If names are not correct, language will not be in accordance with the truth of things.

—Confucius

The language of an African child's formal education was foreign. The language of the books he read was foreign. Thought in him took the visible form of a foreign language... [The] colonial child was made to see the world and where he stands in it as seen and defined by or reflected in the culture of the language of imposition.

—Ngugi Wa Thiong'o

A language is not an umbrella or an overcoat that can be borrowed by unconscious or deliberate mistake, it is like living skin itself.

—Rabindranath Tagore

Language does not extend to explaining the Way in detail, but it can be grasped intuitively.

—Miyamoto Musashi
Go Rin No Sho (The Book of Five Rings), 1645

Language | Western

Bad spellers of the world, untie!

—Graffito

To speak a language is to take on a world, a culture.

—Fanon

Language is the dress of thought.

—Samuel Johnson
"Cowley," Lives of the English Poets, 1781

Colourless green ideas sleep furiously.

—Noam Chomsky
A demonstration of how grammatical structure does not result in meaning

The mystery of language was revealed to me. I knew then that "w-at-e-r" meant the wonderful cool something that was flowing over my hand. That living word awakened my soul, gave it light, joy, set it free!

—Helen Keller
Deaf-blind American author

If thoughts corrupt language, language can also corrupt thought.

—George Orwell

Language is a uniquely human characteristic. Each person has programmed into his genes a faculty called universal grammar.

—Noam Chomsky

Casca: But, for mine own part, it was Greek to me.

—Shakespeare
Julius Caesar

Political language... is designed to make lies sound truthful and murder respectable, and to give the appearance of solidity to pure wind.

—George Orwell
"Politics and the English Language," April 1946,
The Collected Essays, Journalism and Letters of George Orwell

Hazem I. Kira

In general, every country has the language it deserves.

—Jorge Luis Borges

By such innovations are languages enriched, when the words are adopted by the multitude and naturalized by custom.

—Miguel de Cervantes

The fact of the matter is that the "real world" is to a large extent built up on the language habits of the group. No two languages are ever sufficiently similar to be considered as representing the same reality.

—Edward Sapir

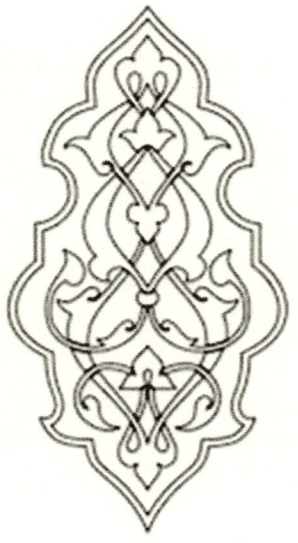

Law and Justice

Law and Justice | Eastern

Who can protest an injustice but does not is an accomplice to the act.

—The Talmud

The more laws and orders are prominent,
The more thieves and bandits there will be.

—Lao Tzu

Justice is the soul of the universe.

—Omar Khayyam

The human intellect delights in inventing specious arguments in order to support injustice [for] itself.

—Mahatma Gandhi

The end of punishment is to make an end of punishing.

—Chinese proverb

And give full measure when you measure out, and weigh with a true balance; this is fair and better in the end.

—Qur'an 17:35

Whoever takes someone's property, or uses him for forced labor, or presses an unjustified claim upon him. It should be known that this is what the Lawgiver had in mind when he forbade injustice.

—Ibn Khaldun
The Muqaddimah, trans. Franz Rosenthal, 2005

My guiding principle will be justice and complete impartiality.

— Jinnah
Presidential address to the Constituent Assembly of Pakistan, August 11, 1947

There is no justice in passing a verdict by relying on probability.

—Ali

Only decide on the basis of proof, be kind to the weak so that they can express themselves freely and without fear, deal on an equal footing with litigants.

—Umar

A just city should favor justice and the just, hate tyranny and injustice, and give them both their just deserts.

—Fârâbi

H. Gibb, "Mazalim," The Dictionary of Islam

Code of Hammurabi (as written on a stone column):
If a noble has destroyed the eye of an aristocrat, his eye shall be destroyed.
If he has destroyed the eye of a commoner, he shall pay one mina of silver.
If he has destroyed the eye of a noble's slave or broken the bone of a noble's slave, he shall pay one half of his value.
If a son has struck his father, they shall cut off his hand.
If a noble charge another noble with murder but fails to prove it, the accuser shall be put to death.
If a married woman shall be caught lying with another man, both shall be bound and thrown into the river.

—Hammurabi

Law and Justice | Western

Judicial decrees may not change the heart, but they can restrain the heartless.
—Martin Luther King Jr.

Society prepares the crime, the criminal commits it.

—Henry Thomas Buckle

Crime is contagious. If the government becomes a lawbreaker, it breeds contempt for law; it invites every man to become a law unto himself.
—Supreme Court Justice Brandeis
Olmstead v. United States

If you tremble indignation at every injustice then you are a comrade of mine.
—Che Guevara

We need to be clear. Cruelty disfigures our national character. It is incompatible with our constitutional order, with our laws, and with our most prized values. Cruelty can be as effective as torture in destroying human dignity, and there is no moral distinction between one and the other. To adopt and apply a policy of cruelty anywhere within this world is to say that our forefathers were wrong about their belief in the rights of man, because there is no more fundamental right than to be safe from cruel and inhumane treatment. Where cruelty exists, law does not.

—Alberto J. Mora

Where there is no law, there is no freedom.

—John Locke

Lawlessness is lawlessness. Anarchy is anarchy is anarchy. Neither race nor color nor frustration is an excuse for either lawlessness or anarchy.

—Thurgood Marshall
Speech, 15 Aug. 1966

XXXIX. No Freeman shall be taken, or imprisoned, or outlawed, or exiled, or in any way harmed, nor will we go upon him, nor will we send upon him, except by the legal judgement of his peers, or by the law of the land.
XL. To none will we sell, to none deny or delay, right or justice.

—Magna Carta, 1215

Nature never breaks her own laws.

—Leonardo da Vinci

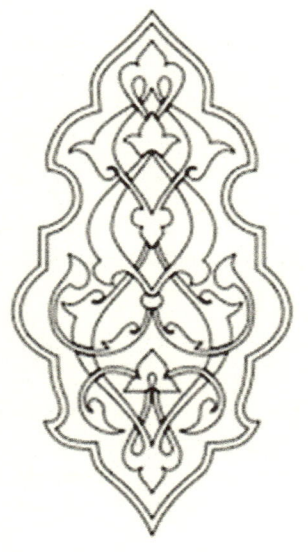

Law and Justice:
Unjust Laws, Civil Disobedience

Law and Justice: Unjust Laws, Civil Disobedience | Eastern

An unjust law is no law at all.

—St. Augustine of Hippo
Letter from Birmingham Jail, April 16, 1963

No one nation should be complainant, prosecutor and judge

—Nelson Mandela
Commonwealth Heads of Government Meeting

I believe in the doctrine of non-violence as a weapon of the stronger.
I believe that a man is the strongest soldier for daring to die unarmed with his breast bare before the enemy.

—Mahatma Gandhi
The World's Great Speeches

Where choice is set between cowardice and violence, I would advise violence...
I prefer to use arms in defense of honor rather than remain the vile witness of dishonor.

—Nelson Mandela
Quoted in Time magazine, January 3, 2000

To indulge in political murder was to sow the dragon's teeth... The proper method to paralyse an oppressive government was to refuse taxes, resign from all services and boycott institutions supporting the government... Such a programme would compel any government to come to terms.

—Abul Kalam Azad
Quoted in Eight Lives: A Study of the Hindu-Muslim Encounter

I have been told that non-cooperation is unconstitutional... On the contrary, I hold that non-cooperation is a just and religious doctrine.

—Mahatma Gandhi
Speech given in 1920 in Madras, India. The World's Great Speeches

Law and Justice: Unjust Laws, Civil Disobedience | Western

I consider myself neither legally nor morally bound to obey the laws made by a body in which I have no representation.

—H. Rap Brown
Statement written in 1967

There is a higher law than the law of government. That's the law of conscience.

—Stokely Carmichael
United Press International dispatch, October 28, 1966

Nonviolent direct action seeks to create such a crisis and foster such a [moral] tension that a community which has constantly refused to negotiate is forced to confront the issue. It seeks to dramatize the issue that it can no longer be ignored [making the status quo untenable]... Actually, we who engage in nonviolent direct action are not the creators of tension. We merely bring to the surface the hidden tension that is already alive.

—Martin Luther King Jr.
Letter from Birmingham Jail, April 16, 1963

Power never takes a back step—only in the face of more power.

—Malcolm X (El-Hajj Malik El-Shabazz)
Malcolm X Speaks, 1965

Liberty

Liberty | Eastern

Freedom and liberty lose out by default because good people are not vigilant.

—Desmond M. Tutu

As quoted in Hope and Suffering: Sermons and Speeches, 1984

Excessive liberty leads to anarchy, and excessive order leads to autocracy.

—Sun Yat-sen

1924 speech quoted in All under Heaven: Sun Yat-sen and His Revolutionary Thought

Our vote is the best guarantee of our civil rights and the best expression of our citizenship.

—Agha K. Saeed

Some who are too scrupulous to steal your possessions nevertheless see no wrong in tampering with your thoughts.

—Kahlil Gibran

Spiritual sayings of Kahlil Gibran

Liberty, democracy, and legality are never condescendingly bestowed gifts. . . Long live the People!

—500 Beijing University Faculty

Statement by 500 Beijing University Faculty on peaceful pro-democracy demonstrations in China, The World's Great Speeches

What difference does it make to the dead, the orphans, and the homeless, whether the mad destruction is wrought under the name of totalitarianism or the holy name of liberty and democracy?

—Mahatma Gandhi

Liberty | Western

I know not what course others may take; but as for me, give me liberty, or give me death!

—Patrick Henry

Liberty, equality, and fraternity.

—French Revolutionary Chant

Liberty is always unfinished business.

—American Civil Liberties Union Annual Report
1955-1956

It is better to die on your feet than to live on your knees.

—Dolores Ibárruri

O Liberté, que de crimes on commet en ton nom!
Oh Liberty, what crimes are committed in thy name!

—Marie-Jeanne Roland

Liberty is the capacity to do anything that does no harm to others.

—The Declaration of Rights of Man and the Citizen
France, Article 4, August 26, 1789

Those who would give up essential Liberty, to purchase a little temporary Safety, deserve neither Liberty not Safety.

—Benjamin Franklin
Reply to Gov. Robert Morris, November 1755

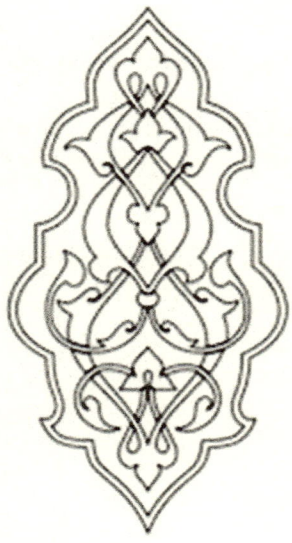

Leadership

Leadership | Eastern

I cannot live without the people, and if ever you begin to doubt me, kill me!
—Alexander Kerensky

A leader leads by example not by force.

—Sun Tzu

[A leader is a] servant of all and a master of none.

—Akbar the Great

Leadership | Western

Each time someone stands for an ideal, or acts to improve the lot of others, or strikes out against injustice, they send forward a ripple of hope.
—Robert F. Kennedy

Ninety percent of leadership is the ability to communicate something people want.

—Dianne Feinstein

Leadership is getting someone else to do what you want him to do because he wants to do it.

—Dwight D. Eisenhower

A leader is a dealer in hope.

—Napoleon Bonaparte

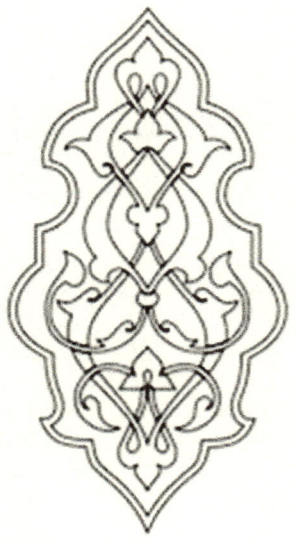

Life and Death

Life and Death | Eastern

I will die, and my ashes will become the spoils of chilly winds.
But even now I shudder at the mere thought of this eventuality.

—Mirza Ghalib
Quoted in Natalia Prigarina, Mirza Ghalib: A Creative Biography

Forget not death, o man! For thou may'st be
Of one thing certain—he forgets not thee.

—Persian Couplet

Welcome death with a smile.

—Iqbal
Rumuz-e-Bekhudi
In Ghulam Sarwar, Islam Beliefs and Teachings

Livelihood like death will reach a man even if the door be closed.

—Persian Couplet

He who gallops with loose rein collides with death.

—Ali
Nahj al-Balagha (Peak of Eloquence)

Death is a bridge that unites the lover with the beloved.

—Kwaja Mamshad Dinwari

A long tongue makes life short.

—Persian proverb

wa-idha-maniyatu anshabat az faraha
alfayta kulla tamimatin lat tanfa'u
When death sinks its claws in,
you find all amulets of no avail.

—Abu Dhu'ayb
Quoted in Heinrich's The Hand of Northwind

It is out of the earth of this country that we were fashioned and it is to this
earth that we shall return.

—Zakir Husain
Quoted in Eight Lives: A Study of the Hindu-Muslim Encounter

Every human being has to meet the end, sweet or sour.

—Ali
Nahj al-Balagha (Peak of Eloquence)

Remember: It is not given to man to take his goods with him.
No one goes away and then comes back.

—Tomb of Egyptian King Inyotef
2600 BC

Death is the means of transitin to future life, which is the ultimate goal of mortal existence.

—Saadia Gaon (Saᵡadiah ben Yosef)

Life and Death | Western

It's not that I'm afraid to die, I just don't want to be there when it happens.

—Woody Allen

The bitterest tear shed over graves are for words left unsaid and deeds left undone.

—Harriet Beecher Stowe
Uncle Tom's Cabin

A life, which does not go into action, is a failure.

—Arnold J. Toynbee

The unexamined life is not worth living.

—Socrates
In Plato's Apology, trans. Benjamin Jowett, 1894

Birth, like death, is a secret of nature.

—Marcus T. Cicero

Life is about becoming more than we are.

—Oprah Winfrey
Charlie Rose television interview, PBS, October 29, 1998

(Life) is unsubstantial, as a dream... But ever and again, a light from above falls into it and then it may become desirable and beautiful.

—Pindar

Cowards die many times before their death,... The valiant never taste of death but one.

—Shakespeare
Julius Ceasar

Oh! Death will find me long before I tire.

—Rupert Brooke
Sonnet, 1908

Pale death, with impartial step, knocks at the poor man's cottage and the palaces of kings.

—Horace

"Master, what gnaws at them so hideously,
their lamentations stun the very air?"
"They have no hope of death," he answered me.

—Dante Alighieri
The Divine Comedy: Inferno, trans. Ciardi Canto

As a well-spent day brings happy sleep,
So a life well used brings happy death.

—Leonardo da Vinci

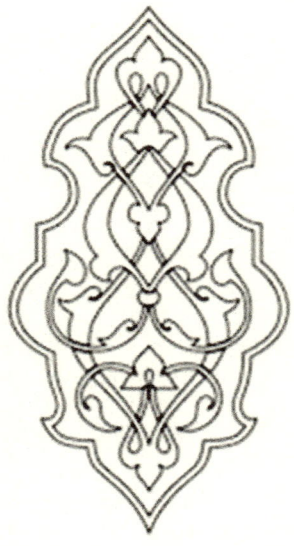

Literature and Writing

Hazem I. Kira

Literature and Writing | Eastern

Let the writer's thought so ripen in thee that it becomes, as it were, thy own thought.

—Chu Hsi

Medicine is my lawful wife and literature is my mistress. When I get tired of one I spend the night with the other.

—Anton Chekhov
Anton Chekhov: Letters on the Short Story, 1964

You cannot open a book without learning something.

—Confucius
The Analects

Literature is the garment which one puts on what he says or writes so that it may appear more attractive.

—Imam Ja'far al-Sadiq
Quoted in Fiqh E Jaferia, The Great Muslim Scientist and
Philosopher Imam Jafar ibn Mohammad As-Sadiq

Do not just read, memorise or imitate, but so that you realise the principle from within your own heart study hard to absorb these things into your body.

—Miyamoto Musashi
Go Rin No Sho (The Book of Five Rings), 1645

What literature needs most to tell and investigate today are humanity's basic fears: the fear of being left outside, and the fear of counting for nothing, and the feelings of worthlessness that come with such fears; the collective humiliations, vulnerabilities, slights, grievances, sensitivities, and imagined insults, and the nationalist boasts and inflations that are their next of kin.

—Orhan Pamuk
Nobel lecture, 2006, as translated by Maureen Freely

The question we writers are asked most often, the favorite question, is: Why do you write? I write because I have an innate need to write. I write because I can't do normal work as other people do. I write because I want to read books like the ones I write. I write because I am angry at everyone. I write because I love sitting in a room all day writing. I write because I can partake of real life only by changing it. I write because I want others, the whole world, to

204

know what sort of life we lived, and continue to live, in Istanbul, in Turkey. I write because I love the smell of paper, pen, and ink. I write because I believe in literature, in the art of the novel, more than I believe in anything else. I write because it is a habit, a passion. I write because I am afraid of being forgotten. I write because I like the glory and interest that writing brings. I write to be alone. Perhaps I write because I hope to understand why I am so very, very angry at everyone. I write because I like to be read. I write because once I have begun a novel, an essay, a page I want to finish it. I write because everyone expects me to write. I write because I have a childish belief in the immortality of libraries, and in the way my books sit on the shelf. I write because it is exciting to turn all life's beauties and riches into words. I write not to tell a story but to compose a story. I write because I wish to escape from the foreboding that there is a place I must go but—as in a dream—can't quite get to. I write because I have never managed to be happy. I write to be happy.

—Orhan Pamuk

Nobel lecture, 2006, as translated by Maureen Freely

Put cotton flake in the inkpot, keep the nib of your pen long, leave space between lines and close up the letters because this is good for the beauty of writing.

—Ali
Nahj al-Balagha (Peak of Eloquence). Ali speaking to his secretary

Literature and Writing | Western

Literature is language charged with meaning.

—Ezra Pound

Books rule the world, or at least those nations which have a written language; the others do not matter.

—Voltaire

I am the sum of my books.

—V. S. Naipaul
Nobel lecture, December 7, 2001

The reading of all good books is like a conversation with all the finest men of past centuries.

—Rene Descartes

To my mind that literature is best and most enduring which is characterized by a noble simplicity.

—Mark Twain
Speech, December 8, 1881

To this day, if you ask me how I became a writer, I cannot give you an answer. To this day, if you ask me how a book is written, I cannot answer. For long periods, if I didn't know that somehow in the past I had written a book, I would have given up.

—V. S. Naipaul
Quoted in "V. S. Naipaul in Search of Himself:
A Conversation with Mel Gussow," New York Times, April 24, 1994

Literature is doomed if liberty of thought perishes.

—George Orwell
"The Prevention of Literature," January 1946, The Collected Essays, Journalism and
Letters of George Orwell

Great literature must spring from an upheaval in the author's soul.

—Robert Benchley

Literature is all that enhances, by means of the word, both your knowledge and your ability to employ that knowledge.

— Samuel Niger

The way to become boring is to say everything.

—Voltaire

Don't get discouraged because there's a lot of mechanical work to writing... I rewrote the first part of A Farewell to Arms at least fifty times... When you first start to write you get all the kick and the reader gets none, but after you learn to work it's your object to convey everything to the reader so that he remembers it not as a story he has read but something that has happened to himself. That is the true test of writing.

—Ernest Hemingway

Loneliness

Hazem I. Kira

Loneliness | Eastern

Ever since I was separated from you my eyes darkened;
the clouds of my eyes pour rain.

—Shams of Tabriz
Rumi's Sun: The Teachings of Shams of Tabriz, 2008

If you are afraid of loneliness, do not marry.

—Anton Chekhov

Loneliness | Western

I lie here buried alive in my loneliness.

—Friedrich Nietzsche
My Sister and I, trans. Oscar Levy, 1951

People are lonely because they build walls instead of bridges.

—J. F. Newton

Loneliness is now so widespread it has become, paradoxically, a shared experience.

—Alvin Toffler
The Third Wave, 1980

Pray that your loneliness may spur you into finding something to live for,
great enough to die for.

—Dag Hammarskjold

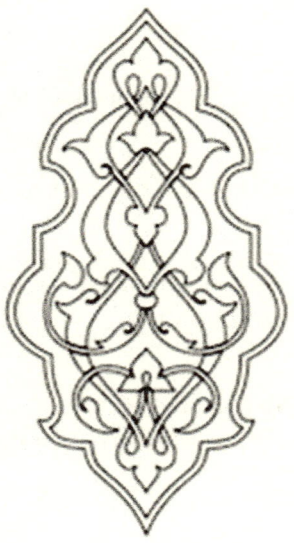

Love

Love | Eastern

He who does not love does not know God.

—Christian proverb

The minute I heard my first love story
I started looking for you,
not knowing
how blind I was
Lovers don't finally meet somewhere
They're in each other all along

—Rumi

Let your love be like the misty rain, coming softly, but flooding the river.
—Madagascan proverb

Women prefer poverty with love to luxury without it.
—The Talmud

I went to a wilderness, love had rained and had covered earth, as feet penetrate
snow, I found my feet covered with love.

—Bayazid Bastami

In Payam-e-Mushriq, Iqbal has Rumi and Goethe meeting in paradise, and
Goethe tells Rumi about the pact between the Doctor Faustus and the Devil.
Rumi responds to him this way:
"Not all can learn love's secret lore,
Not all can enter its high shrine
One only knows by grace divine
That wisdom is the Devil's own,
While Love belongs to man alone."

—Iqbal
Payam-i-Mashriq, trans. Hadi Hussain

Good is stronger than evil; love is stronger than hate; light is stronger than
darkness; life is stronger than death. Victory is ours, through him who
loves us.

—Desmond Tutu

Being deeply loved by someone gives you strength; loving someone deeply gives you courage.

—Lao Tzu

No one is born hating another person because of the colour of his skin, or his background, or his religion. People must learn to hate, and if they can learn to hate, they can be taught to love, for love comes more naturally to the human heart than its opposite.

—Nelson Mandela
Long Walk to Freedom

We will depart, but the eternal nature of love will remain unchanged.
Is there any loss to the sea, if a boat has perished in the deep?

—Mirza Ghalib
Quoted in Natalia Prigarina, Mirza Ghalib: A Creative Biography

Where there is love there is life.

—Mahatma Gandhi

1. Listen to the reed [flute] and the tale it tells,
how it sings of separation:
2. Ever since they cut me from the reed bed,
my wail has caused men and women to weep.
3. I want a heart that is torn open with longing
so that I might share the pain of this love.
4. Whoever has been parted from his source
longs to return to that state of union.
5. At every gathering I play my lament. I'm a friend to both happy and sad.
6. Each befriended me for his own reasons,
yet none searched out the secrets I contain.
7. My secret is not different than my lament,
yet this is not for the senses to perceive.
8. The body is not hidden from the soul,
nor is the soul hidden from the body, and yet the soul is not for everyone to see.

—Rumi
Kabir Helminski, The Rumi Collection:
An Anthology of Translations of Mevlana Jalaluddin Rumi

Love | Western

He whom love touches does not walks in darkness.

—Plato
Symposium, trans. Benjamin Jowett

L'amour est aveugle; l'amitie ferme les yeux.
Love is blind; friendship closes its eyes.

—French proverb

Love is ever the beginning of knowledge as fire is of light.

—Thomas Carlyle
Essays on Goethe

One word
Frees us of all the weight and pain of life:
That word is love.

—Sophocles
Oedipus at Colonus

All the affectionate feelings of a man for others are an extension of his feelings for himself.

—Aristotle
Nicomachean Ethics, 9.8, trans. J. A. K. Thomson, 1953

Not Man alone, but all that roam the wood,
Or wing the sky, or roll along the flood,
Each loves itself, but not itself alone.

—Alexander Pope
An Essay on Man, 3.119, 1734

Love seeks not to possess, but to be possessed.

—R. H. Benson

Gather the rose of love whilst yet is time.

—Edmund Spenser

True love is like seeing ghosts: we all talk about it, but few of us have ever seen one.
—La Rochefoucauld
Maxims, 76, 1665, trans. Louis Kronenberger, 1959

With the lover it is the end which is fixed, the path may be modified indefinitely.
—William James
James's Principles of Psychology

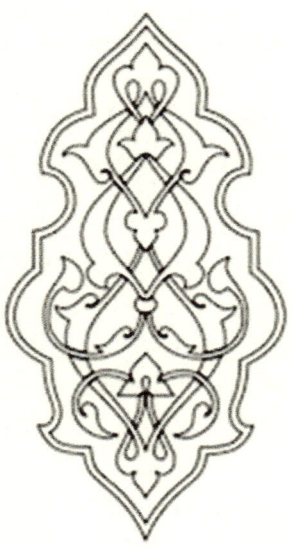

Lust

Lust | Eastern

Those born blind cannot see; similarly blind are those in the grip of lust.

—Chanakya

Intoxication filled the cups. Youth's frenzy took me by the hand. The yielding heart imagined that the path shown by desire and lust led to the destination... each glance annihilating one's resistance.

—Abul Kalam Azad

An enemy to whom you show kindness becomes your friend, excepting lust, the indulgence of which increases its enmity.

—Sa'di

Lust | Western

Capricious, wanton, bold, and brutal lust is meanly selfish; when resisted, cruel; and, like the blast of pestilential winds, taints the sweet bloom of nature's fairest forms.

—John Milton

Their insatiable lust for power is only equaled by their incurable impotence in exercising it.

—Winston Churchill

The difficulty lies, in finding out an exact measure; but eat for necessity, not pleasure, for lust knows not where necessity ends.

—Benjamin Franklin

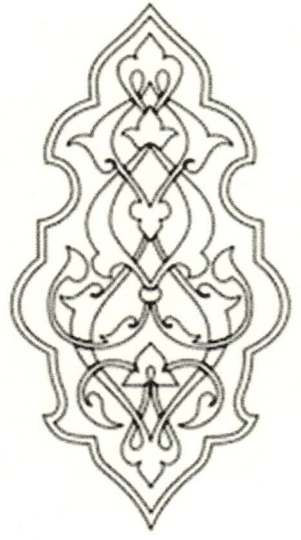

Lying and Deceit

Lying and Deceit | Eastern

Lying to ourselves is more deeply ingrained than lying to others.

—Fyodor Dostoyevsky

What is evil? Killing is evil, lying is evil, slandering is evil, abuse is evil, gossip is evil: envy is evil, hatred is evil, to cling to false doctrine is evil; all these things are evil. And what is the root of evil? Desire is the root of evil, illusion is the root of evil.

—Buddha

In the war between falsehood and truth, falsehood wins the first battle and truth the last.

—Sheikh Mujibur Rahman
Quoted in Newsweek, January 24, 1972

Hold always the sign of blood in horror. Take care not to shed or stain thyself with it, for the mark is never washed away.

—Saladin
Advice to his son, Dhahir, on an appointment as governor of Aleppo

Little children do not lie till they are taught to do so.

—Saadia Gaon (Saadiah ben Yosef)

el-kezb ma loosh reglein
Lying has no legs [lying will eventually expose itself].

—Egyptian proverb

Lying and Deceit | Western

God has given you one face and you make yourselves another.

—Shakespeare
Hamlet

O, What a tangled web we weave,
When first we practice to deceive!

—Walter Scott

Truly, to tell lies is not honorable;
But when the truth entails tremendous ruin,
To speak dishonorably is pardonable.

—Sophocles
Creusa

You can fool some of the people all of the time, and all of the people some of time, but you cannot fool all of the people all the time.

—Abraham Lincoln

If a man deceives me once, shame on him; if he deceives me twice, shame on me.

—English language proverb

A liar will not be believed, even when he speaks the truth.

—Aesop
"The Shepherd's Boy," Fables, trans. Joseph Jacobs, 1894

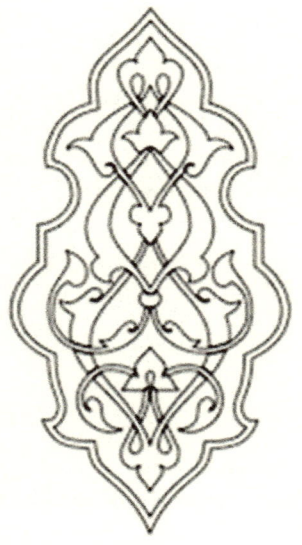

Men and Women

Men and Women | Eastern

Women can't forgive failure

—Anton Chekhov
The Seagull

Let there be spaces in your togetherness.

—Kahlil Gibran

That male and female should dwell together is the greatest of human relations.
—Mencius

The word "shams" (sun) is feminine, and "qamar" (moon) is masculine. The sun burns itself out to give light and life to everything around, and the moon is muneer, meaning it reflects the light. Within itself it has no light; it radiates the brilliance of the sun. So when we shine as men, the implication is that we are reflecting the glorious light of our women."
—Shayk Abdullah Adhami

Men are cruel, but man is kind.

—Rabindranath Tagore

Man is man's mirror.

—Turkish proverb

Surely God's favour is on him bestowed
Whose wife makes glad and prosperous his abode.

—Sa'di
Quoted in A Few Flowers from the Garden of Saadi Shirazi

Men and Women | Western

The way to get most husbands to do something is to suggest that perhaps they're too old to do it.

—Shirley MacLaine

I generally had to give in.

—Napoleon Bonaparte
On his relationship with Josephine, May 19, 1816

If particular care and attention is not paid to the ladies we are determined to foment a rebellion, and will not hold ourselves bound by any laws in which we have no voice or representation.

—Abigail Adams
Letter to John Adams, March 31, 1776

Man has will—but woman has her way!

—Oliver Wendell Holmes Sr.
The Autocrat of the Breakfast Table, 1858

Women lie about their age; men about their income.

—William Feather

In politics, if you want anything said, ask a man. If you want anything done, ask a woman.

—Margaret Thatcher
In "The Touch Top Tory in Britain Wants To Be 'Madame P. M.,'" People, September 15, 1975

Man is the measure of all things.

—Protagoras
As quoted in Plato's Theaetetus, trans. Benjamin Jowett, 1894

There are three classes of men—lovers of wisdom, lovers of honor, lovers of gain.

—Plato
The Republic, trans. Benjamin Jowett

Women always worry about the things that men forget; men always worry about the things women remember... If women didn't exist, all the money in the world would have no meaning.

—Aristotle Onassis
Attributed

Man is very much a creature of habit.

—Alexander Hamilton
In The Federalist Papers, 27, December 25, 1787

Man is neither villain nor hero; he is rather both villain and hero.

—Martin Luther King Jr.
Strength to Love

'Tis strange what a man may do, and a woman yet think him an angel.

—W. M. Thackeray

Mothers don't see the man, only the boy.

—Anonymous

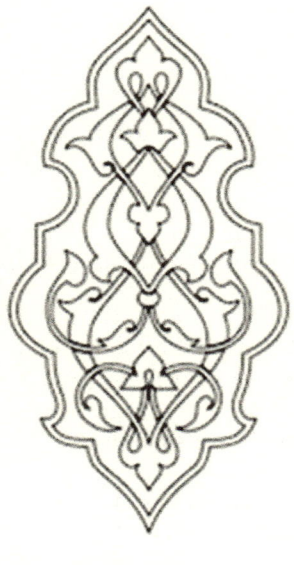

Mercy

Mercy | Eastern

Blessed are the merciful.

—Christian Scriptural proverb

Recompense injury with kindness.

—Lao Tsu

Indeed, before Allah (God) created the creation, He decreed for Himself, "Indeed My Mercy prevails over My Anger."

—Muhammad
Sahih al-Bukhari

Mercy| Western

Yet I shall temper so
Justice with Mercy.

—John Milton
Paradise Lost, 10.77, 1667

Dost thou wish to receive mercy? Show Mercy to thy neighbor.

—St. John Chrysostom

Portia: The quality of mercy is not strain'd;
It droppeth as the gentle rain from heaven
Upon the place beneath: it is twice bless'd
It blesseth him that gives and him that takes.

—Shakespeare
The Merchant of Venice

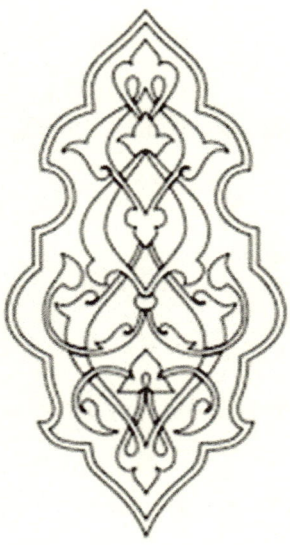

Mistakes

Mistakes | Eastern

Saru mo ki kara ochiru.
Even monkeys fall from trees.

—Japanese proverb

No matter how far you have gone on a wrong road, turn back.

—Turkish proverb

The greatest glory in living lives is not in never falling, but in rising every time we fall.

—Nelson Mandela
Long Walk to Freedom

Take warning by the misfortunes of others, that others may not take example from you.

—Sa'di

Tolerance blinds the eye to mistakes,
but angry looks reveal even the smallest fault.

—Shams of Tabriz
Rumi's Sun: The Teachings of Shams of Tabriz, 2008

Sweep the snow from thine own door: spy not at the frost on another's tiles.

—Chinese proverb

Who stands still in mud sticks in it.

—Chinese proverb

Mistakes | Western

Only those who do nothing... make no mistakes.

—Joseph Conrad
An Outcast of the Islands, 3.2, 1896

What should happen when you make a mistake is this: you take your knocks, you learn your lessons, and then you move on.

—Ronald Reagan
Television broadcast, March 4, 1987

It is a woeful mistake to suppose that the educated are kinder or more tolerant.

—Namier

Men may be as positive in error as in truth.

—John Locke

Opportunity

Opportunity | Eastern

How long will you keep pounding on an open door. Begging for someone to open it?

—Rabia al-Adawiyyah

Opportunities multiply as they are seized.

—Sun Tzu
The Art of War

Opportunity passes away like the cloud. Therefore, make use of good opportunities.

—Ali
Nahj al-Balagha (Peak of Eloquence)

To make haste before the proper time or delay after a proper opportunity, in either case is folly.

—Ali
Nahj al-Balagha (Peak of Eloquence)

Winnow while the wind is blowing.

—Japanese proverb

Opportunity | Western

Timid men are more likely to be moved to trepidation than daring in the face of great opportunities.

—Henry Kissinger
A World Restored: Metternich, Castlereagh and the Problems of Peace

As the Wind blows you must set your sail.

—Thomas Fuller

Make hay while the sun shineth.

—John Clarke

We are a nation of immigrants. It is immigrants who brought to this land the skills of their hands and brains to make it a beacon of opportunity and of hope for all men.

—H.H. Lehman
House Sub-Committee on Immigration and Naturalization

Opportunity is missed by most people because it's dressed in overalls and looks like work.

—Thomas Edison

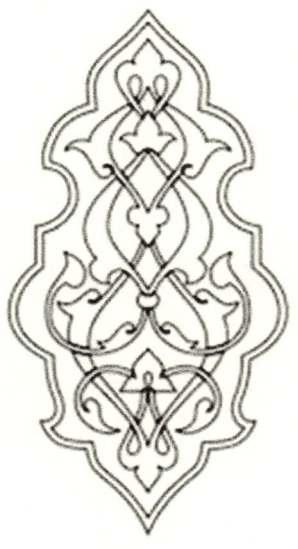

Order

Order | Eastern

To put the nation in order, we must put the family in order; to put the family in order we must cultivate our personal life; and to cultivate our personal life, we must first set our hearts right.

—Confucius
The Analects

Anticipate the difficult by managing the easy.

—Lao Tzu
Quoted in Pebbles, Pearls and Gems of the Orient, 1882

Order | Western

Order is Heaven's first law.

—Alexander Pope

A. A violent order is disorder; and
B. A great disorder is an order.
These Two things are one.

—Wallace Stevens
Connoisseur of Chaos," Parts of a World, 1942

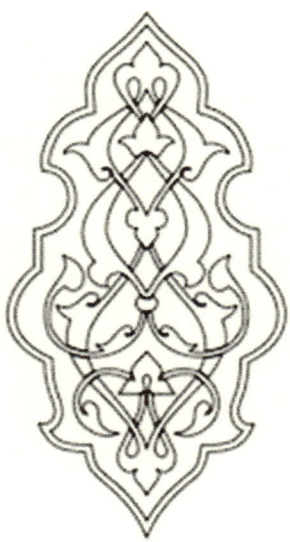

Patience

Patience | Eastern

Winter always turns to spring.

—Nichiren

A gem is not polished without rubbing, nor is a man perfected without trials.

—Chinese proverb

Patience is of two kinds, over what pains you, and patience against what you covet.

—Ali

A shy person cannot learn, and an impatient person cannot teach.

—Pirkei Avot

Patience is the key to release.

—Arabic proverb

Dhu-l-nun asked, "What is the end of love?" he was told, "O simpleton, love has no end because the Beloved has no end."

—Dhu-l-nun

Patience | Western

These are the times that try men's souls. The summer soldier and the sunshine patriot will, in this crisis, shrink from the service of their country; but he that stands it now, deserves the love and thanks of man and woman.

—Thomas Paine
The Crisis, December 1776

Patience breaks iron.

—German proverb

Patience is the greatest of all virtues.

—Dionysius Cato

Patience is the best remedy for every trouble.

—Plautus
Rudens

Patience and diligence, like faith, move mountains.

—William Penn
Some Fruits of Solitude, 234, 1693

Upon the heat and flame of thy distemper
Sprinkle cool patience.

—Shakespeare
Hamlet

Peace, security, and diplomacy

Peace, security, and diplomacy | Eastern

In peace prepare for war, in war prepare for peace.

—Sun Tzu

This may not be a just peace, but it is more just than the continuation of war.
—Alija Izetbegović
Quoted on BBC News

All diplomacy is a continuation of war by other means.

—Chou En-Lai
Interview with Edgar Snow, Saturday Evening Post, March 27, 1954 (cf. Clausewitz)

When your heart is ready, peace will come looking for you.

—Ajahn Chah
Reflections, 107, 1994

Blessed are the peacemakers.

—Christian proverb

Peace is indivisible.

—Maxim Litvinov
Note to the Allies, February 25, 1920; A. U. Pope Maxim Litvinoff, 1943

Settlement can only be achieved between equals.

—Jinnah
The Tasks Ahead—Speech at a rally at the University Stadium, Lahore, October 30, 1947

Every lover of peace must emphasize similarities.

—Abul Kalam Azad
Quoted in Eight Lives: A Study of the Hindu-Muslim Encounter

Sincere diplomacy is no more possible than dry water or wooden iron.

—Joseph Stalin

Let the strivings of us all, prove Martin Luther King Jr. to have been correct, when he said that humanity can no longer be tragically bound to the starless midnight of racism and war... Let a new age dawn!

—Nelson Mandela
Acceptance address for Nobel Peace Prize, December 10, 1993

Lead me from despair to hope, from fear to trust.
Lead me from hate to love, from war to peace.
Let peace fi ll our heart, our world, our universe.

—Satish Kumar
"Prayers for Peace," 1981; adapted from the Upanishads

Sublime is the moment
When the world is at peace
And the limitless deep
Lies bated in the morning sun.

—Hirohito
*Untitled poem. In Robert Trumball, "A Leader Who Took Japan to War, to Surrender,
and Finally to Peace," New York Times, January 7, 1989*

Peace, Security, and Diplomacy | Western

They make a wilderness and call it peace

—Tacitus

True peace is not merely the absence of tension; it is the presence of justice.
—Martin Luther King Jr.

Mother Courage: Don't tell me peace has broken out—I've gone and brought
all these supplies!

—Bertolt Brecht
Mother Courage, 8, 1939, trans. Eric Bentley, 1955

I am tired of fighting, our chiefs are killed... it is cold and we have no
blankets. The little children are freezing to death... hear me, my chiefs, I am
tired: my heart is sick and sad. From where the sun now stands... I will fight
no more forever.

—Chief Joseph

Those who make peaceful revolution impossible will make violent revolution
inevitable.

—John Fitzgerald "Jack" Kennedy

All we are saying is give peace a chance.

—John Lennon

I am convinced that if this peace is not made on the highest principles of justice, it will be swept away by the peoples of the world in less than a generation.

—Woodrow Wilson
Remarks to associates in 1919 on what to do with the land of the dissolving Ottoman Empire.
Quoted in David Fromkin, Peace to End All Peace

Peace and justice are two sides of the same coin.

—Dwight D. Eisenhower

Peace depends ultimately not on political arrangement but on the conscience of mankind.

—Henry A. Kissinger

Peace hath her victories
No less renown'd than war.

—John Milton
"Sonnet 16," 1.10, May 1952

Peace is the aim of the world… justice is the way to attain it.

—Martin Buber
Letter to Mohandas K. Gandhi, 1939. In Allen and Linda Kirschner, eds.,
Blessed Are the Peacemakers, 2, 1971

Princess Isabelle: The king desires peace.
William Wallace: Longshanks desires peace?
Princess Isabelle: He declares it to me, I swear it. He proposes that you withdraw your attack. In return he grants you title, estates, and this chest of gold which I am to pay to you personally.
William Wallace: A lordship and titles. Gold. That I should become Judas?
Princess Isabelle: Peace is made in such ways.
William Wallace: Slaves are made in such ways.

—Braveheart, 1995

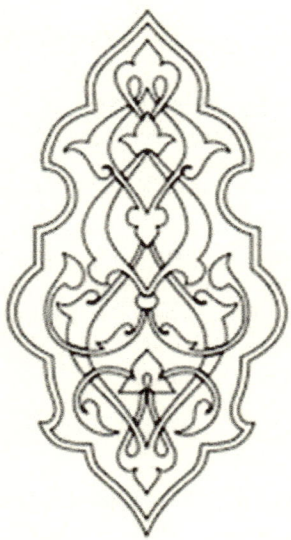

Poetry

Poetry | Eastern

A poet's autobiography is his poetry.

—Yevgeny Yevtushenko

Poetry is like a bird, it ignores all frontiers.

—Yevegeny Yevtushenko

Portrayer of the inmost soul
Of poetry, whose efforts goal.

—Iqbal
Payam-i-Mashriq, trans. Hadi Hussain

My thought fills the rose petal with colour.
Every line I write is a drop of my own blood.
Lest thou hold poetry to be madness,
Know that the perfection of madness is the fullness of wisdom.
I am made rich with talent,
But in the land of Ind I am disgraced.
The luckless rose and tulip hear not my song;
I, a song-bird, am a stranger in my own rose-garden.
Since fate must favour the ignoble and the base,
Woe to the man who is a man of merit!

—Iqbal
Mohammed Iqbal, Poet and Philosopher, trans. Mumtaz Hasan

In poetry I am the pupil of the Most Benevolent and I dispel the obscurity of meaning by the glitter of the pearl of my talent.

—Mirza Ghalib

Poetry | Western

Poetic license may be forgiven to the tellers of unusual storeis.

—Eliphas Levi

I will not make a poem nor the least part of a poem but has reference to the soul,
Because having look'd at the objects of the universe, I find there is no one nor any particle of one but has a reference to the soul.

—Walt Whitman
"Starting from Paumanok" (12), 1860, Leaves of Grass

My poems are hymns of praise to the glory of life.

—Edith Sitwell
"Some Notes on My Poetry," Collected Poems, 1954

A poem should not mean but be.

—Archibald MacLeish
Ars Peotica, 1926

Modern poets add a lot of water to their ink.

—Goethe

One merit of poetry few persons will deny: it says more and in fewer words than prose.

—Voltaire

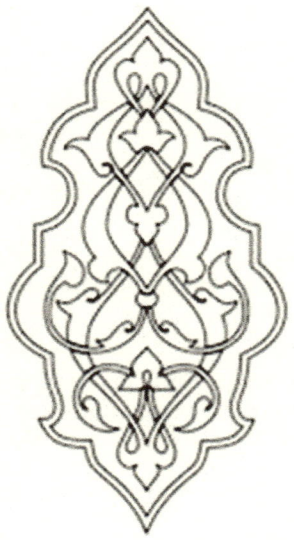

Politics

Politics | Eastern

Politicians are the same all over. They promise to build bridges, even where there are no rivers.

—Nikita Khrushchev

All reactionaries are paper tigers.

—Mao Zedong

Asked by the King why God had created flies, Ja'far replied: God had created the flies in order to humble the pride of tyrannical and despotic rulers.

—Ja'far al-Sadiq

I consider it completely unimportant who in the party will vote, or how; but what is extraordinarily important is this—who will count the votes, and how.

—Joseph Stalin
As quoted in The Memoirs of Stalin's Former Secretary, Boris Bazhanov, 1992

We should have a state in which we could live and breathe as free men and which we could develop according to our own lights and culture.

—Jinnah

If the United States of America or Britain is having elections, they don't ask for observers from Africa or from Asia. But when we have elections, they want observers.

—Nelson Mandela

He who pays the piper calls the tune.

—Anonymous

Politics | Western

Do not put such unlimited power into the hands of husbands. Remember all men would be tyrants if they could.

—Abigail Adams

I recognize no moral law in politics. Politics is a game... in which the rules are constantly being changed by the players to suit themselves.

—Adolph Hitler
Remark to the author. In Hermann Rauschning, The Voice of Destruction, 1940

Power tends to corrupt and absolute power corrupts absolutely.

—Lord Acton

Renunciation of world politics offers no protection from its consequences.

—Oswald Spengler
The People, Yes, 1936

Let us therefore boldly define a political system as any persistent pattern of human relationships that involves, to a significant extent, control, influence, power, or authority.

—Robert A. Dahl
Modern Political Analysis

There is no morality in politics; there is only expediency.

—Lenin
Speech, September 1915

Money is the mother's milk of politics.

—Jesse Unruh
Speaker of the California State Assembly. His signature saying

Politics makes strange bedfellows.

—Charles Dudley Warner
"Fifteenth Week," My Summer in a Garden, 1871

Hamlet: A politician... one that would circumvent God.

—Shakespeare
Hamlet

All political systems undergo change.

—Robert A. Dahl
Modern Political Analysis

Decide exactly what you have to achieve. Do you want to help people, or do you want to be powerful?

—Mario Cuomo

Thrasymachus that Socrates purported to attack. Thrasymachus had said (according to Plato):
"I say that the just is nothing else than the advantage of the stronger... Do you not know... that some cities are ruled by a despot, others by the people, and others again by the aristocracy?.
The art of government is to make two-thirds of the people pay all it possibly can for the benefit of the other third.

—Voltaire

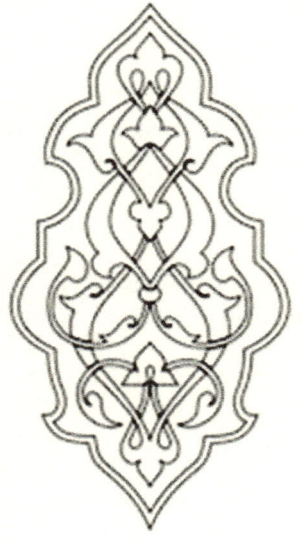

Politics: Nations and National Identity

Politics: Nations and National Identity | Eastern

No nation can find its own salvation by breaking away from others.

—Mahatma Gandhi

The individual derives his honor from his nation
A nation is organized when the individuals are united together.

—Iqbal
Quoted in Iqbal Review, vol. 2, Iqbal Academy, 1961

No nation can rise to the height of glory unless your women are side by side with you.

—Jinnah

We should begin to work in that spirit and in course of time all these angularities of the majority and minority communities will vanish.

—Jinnah
Presidential address to the Constituent Assembly of Pakistan, August 11, 1947

The Chinese people have only family and clan solidarity; they do not have national spirit... they are just a heap of loose sand... Other men are the carving knife and serving dish; we are the fish and the meat.

—Sun Yat-sen
China as a Heap of Loose Sand

We should have a State in which we could live and breathe as free men and which we could develop according to our own lights and culture.

—Jinnah

Nationalism is sometimes a combination of culture as identity and culture as communication.

—Ali A. and Alamin M. Mazrui
The Power of Babel: Language and Governance in the African Experience

Nationalism is sometimes a combination of culture as identity and culture as communication. When nationalism and the language are either completely or substantially fused, what we get is linguistic nationalism, with its focus on pride in one's language.

—Ali Mazrui
The Power of Babel: Language and Governance in the African Experience

Gentlemen, each one of you is one of the 400,000,000; and you personally should assume this responsibility [to make China a world leader]. But your first step is to revive the spirit of nationalism.

—Sun Yat-sen
1924 speech, The World's Great Speeches

Can a nation be free if it oppresses other nations? It cannot.

—Lenin

The ruin of a nation begins in the homes of its people.

—Ashanti African proverb

I deem it my national, religious and human duty to liberate my country and my people from servitude.

—Abul Kalam Azad
Quoted in Eight Lives: A Study of the Hindu-Muslim Encounter

Dead men have no passports.

—Anonymous

Politics: Nations and National Identity | Western

The great nations have always acted like gangsters, and the small nations like prostitutes.

—Stanley Kubrick
In Guardian, June 5, 1963

A nation is judged by the character of her citizens.

—Charles C. Parks
In an address at the Union League Club on Washington's Birthday, 1904

My country is mankind.

—Tom Paine

Nations are imagined political communities.

—Benedict Anderson
Imagined Communities: Reflections on the Origin and Spread of Nationalism

[God] has given us the world only as a place of exile, and not as our true country.
—Pope Leo XIII
erum Novarum, On the Condition of Workers, May 15, 1891

An immoral nation invites its own ruin.
—Dwight D. Eisenhower
"Some Thoughts on the Presidency," Reader's Digest, November 1968

In the last analysis the all-important factor in national greatness is national character.
—Theodore Roosevelt

Linguistic nationalism is the version of nationalism that is concerned about the value of its own language, that seeks to defend it against other languages, and that encourages its use.
—Ali Mazrui
Ethnicity in Bondage: Is Its Liberation Premature? Keynote address, UNRISD/UNDP International Seminar on Ethnic Diversity and Public Policies (New York, August 17-19, 1994)

The abiding purpose of every nationalist is to secure more power and more prestige, not for himself but for the nation or other unit in which he has chose to sink his own individuality.
—George Orwell
"Notes on Nationalism," May 1945, The Collected Essays, Journalism and Letters of George Orwell, vol. 3, Sonia Orwell and Ian Angus, eds., 1968

Tutto nello Stato, niente al di fuori dello Stato, nulla contro lo Stato.
Everything in the State, nothing outside the State, nothing against the State.
—Mussolini
In a speech delivered on October 28, 1925

Politics: Governance and Governments

Politics: Governance and Governments | Eastern

If the cat is away, the mice will play.

—Egyptian proverb

The most miserable rulers are those whose purses are fat and their people thin.

—Salahdin

To rule with equity is like the north star, which is fixed, and all the rest go around it.

—Confucius

In the construction of a country, it is not the practical workers but the idealists and planners that are difficult to find.

—Sun Yat-sen
Chung-shan Ch'üan-shu (Zhongshan Quanshu), vol. II

Who can govern himself is fi t to govern the world.

—Chinese proverb

I hold out a hand of friendship to the leaders of all parties and their members, and ask all of them to join us in working together to tackle the problems we face as a nation

—Nelson Mandela
Victory speech, 1994

Be kind to those under you and treat them well.

—Abu Bakr
In Ghulam Sarwar, Islam Beliefs and Teaching

Out of your hours of work, fi x a time for the complainants and for those who want to approach you with their grievances. During this time you should do no other work but hear them and pay attention to their complaints and grievances... Do not let your army and police be in the audience hall at such times so that those who have grievances against your regime may speak to you freely, unreservedly and without fear.

—Ali
Nahj al-Balagha (Peak of Eloquence), Letter 53

Give what is right and take what is right. Trust produces trust. Follow it strictly and do not be one of those who fail to discharge it.

—Uthman ibn Affan
In Ghulam Sarwar, Islam Beliefs and Teaching

[The greatest impediment to scientific progress (in Egypt) are] bureaucracy and legal rigidity, which are the enemies of a creative mind.

—Ahmed Zewail
Interview with Aziza Sami. "Clash of Words." Al-Ahram Weekly Online, no. 573, February 14-20, 2002.

Lead the people by regulations, keep them in order by punishments (hsing), and they will flee from you and lose all self-respect. But lead them by virtue and keep them in order by established morality (li), and they will keep their self-respect and come to you.

—Confucius
Analetics, XII

Politics: Governance and Governments | Western

Suppose I am a crook, and suppose I am a congressman, but I repeat myself.
—Mark Twain
Quoted in Restoration: Congress, Term Limits and the Recovery of Deliberative Democracy

It is much safer for a prince to be feared than loved.

—Machiavelli

Power must never be trusted without a check.

—John Adams
In a letter to Jefferson, February 2, 1816

It was once said that the moral test of government is how that government treats those who are in the dawn of life, the children; those who are in the twilight of life, the elderly and those who are in the shadows of life—the sick, the needy and the handicapped.

—Vice President Hubert Humphrey
Speech at dedication of Hubert H. Humphrey Building, Washington DC, November 1977

No government can stand which is not founded upon justice.

—Aristotle
Politics, 7.14, trans. Benjamin Jowett, 1855

Conduct lies in masterful administration of the unforeseen.

—Robert Bridges

A government of laws and not men.

—John Adams

Of government interference: Laissez faire, lasses passer. Leave it alone, and let it happen.

—Francois Quesnay

The punishment which the wise suffer who refuse to take part in the government, is to live under the government of worse men.

—Plato

A free government is a complicated piece of machinery, the nice and exact adjustment of whose springs, wheels, and weights, is not yet well comprehended by the artists of the age, and still less by the people.

—John Adams
Letter from John Adams to Thomas Jefferson

The administration of justice is the firmest pillar of Government.

—George Washington

I have nothing but contempt for the kind of governor who is afraid, for whatever reason, to follow the course that he knows is best for the State.

—Sophocles
Antigon

Government is not reason; it is not eloquence; it is force. Like fire, it is a dangerous servant and a fearful master.

—George Washington

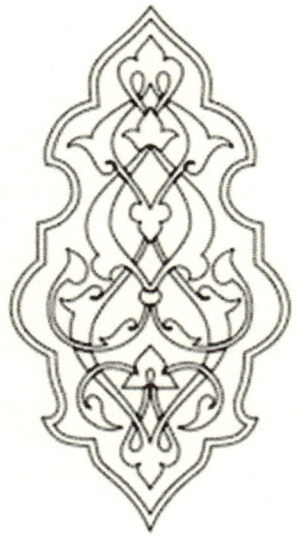

Politics: Democracy

Politics: Democracy | Eastern

Comrades!... I remain a republican... May I trust you as I trust myself?
—Alexander Kerensky
In a 1917 speech by the ruler of new Russian Republic
before it was displaced by the Bolshevist dictatorship, The World's Great Speeches

Since the end of the World War II, there have been two movements for democracy: one for democracy inside each nation, and second for democracy among nations. The second movement insists upon sovereign equality among all nations, large and small, rich and poor, developed and developing.
—Agha K. Saeed

The spirit of democracy cannot be imposed from without.
—Mahatma Gandhi

You have to stand guard over the development and maintenance of democracy... in your own native soil.
—Jinnah
Address to the officers in Malir, Karachi

Democracy demands discipline, tolerance and mutual regard.
—Jawaharlal Nehru

History teaches that no oppressed class has ever come into power and cannot come into power, without passing through a period of dictatorship... [&] that the most democratic bourgeois republic is nothing more than a machine for the suppression of the working class by the bourgeoisie.
—Nikolai Lenin
In a speech titled the "Dictatorship of the Proletariat," The World's Great Speeches

Politics: Democracy | Western

There never was a democracy yet that did not commit suicide.
—John Adams
Letter to John Taylor, April 15, 1814

The most natural and human government is that of consent.
—William Penn

The most may err as grossly as the few.

John Dryden

Constitutional government in which men are citizens is one under which each individual obeys himself when he obeys the law, and so remains quite free.
—Rousseau

[An Illiberal democracy is one in which] democratically elected regimes, often re-elected or reaffirmed through referenda, but who routinely ignore constitutional limits on their power and deprive their citizens of basic rights.
—Fareed Zakaria

The Future of Freedom: Illiberal Democracy at Home and Abroad, 2003 That this nation, under God, shall have a new birth of freedom, and that government of the people, by the people, for the people, shall not perish from the earth.
—Abraham Lincoln
Speech at Gettysburg, November 19, 1863

We appealed to those [laws] of nature, and found them engraved on our heats.
—Thomas Jefferson
Letter to John Hambden Pleasants, April 19, 1824

Freedom is not a gift bestowed upon us by other men, but a right that belongs to us by the laws of God and nature.

—Benjamin Franklin

[Just government] derives its moral authority from God.

—Antonio Scalia

The sacred rights of mankind are not to be rummaged for among old parchments or musty records. They are written as with the sunbeam, in the whole volume of human nature, by the hand of Divinity itself, and can never be erased or obscured by mortal power.

—Alexander Hamilton
"The Farmer Refuted," American State Papers, 1775

The state of nature has a law of nature to govern it, which obliges every one: and reason, which is that law, teaches all mankind... no one ought to harm another in his life, health, liberty, or possessions: for men being all the workmanship of one omnipotent and infinitely wise Maker.

—John Locke
Two Treatises of Government, 1690

We hold these truths to be self-evident, that all men are created equal, that they are endowed by their Creator with certain unalienable Rights, that among these are Life, Liberty and the pursuit of happiness.

—The American Declaration of Independence

Praise

Praise | Eastern

He who drops his head hearing praise, and is glad to be told of his faults, is a sage.

—Chinese proverb

When the heart is sound, it is indifferent to whether anyone praises or blames it... and to whether anyone accepts it or rejects it.

—Jilani
The Removal of Cares

Neither the beauty of your speech,... nor the praise of an ignorant man... nor even your own convictions.... are reasons to be proud.

—Sa'di
Gulistan

Many a man gets into mischief because of being spoken well about.

—Ali (Ali ibn Talib)
Nahj al-Balagha (Peak of Eloquence)

Praise | Western

But when I tell him he hates flatters,
He says he does, being then most flattered.

—Shakespeare

I suppose flattery hurts no one, that is, if he doesn't inhale.

—Adlai Stevenson

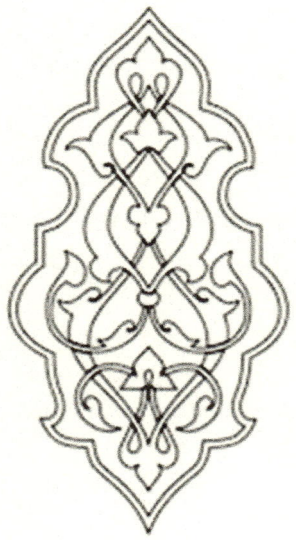

Prejudice

Prejudice | Eastern

We must distinguish the prejudices of the ignorant, which is relatively much easier to remedy, from the prejudices of the learned.

—Agha K. Saeed
Quoted in Encyclopedia of Capitalism

People are enemies of what they do not know.

—Ali
Nahj al-Balagha (Peak of Eloquence)

Even now there are some states in existence where there are discriminations made and bars imposed against a particular class.

—Jinnah
Presidential address to the Constituent Assembly, August 11, 1947

Prejudice | Western

We all decry prejudice, yet are all prejudiced.

—Herbert Spencer
Social Statics, 2.17.2, 1851

All I care to know is that a man is a human being—that is enough for me; he can't be any worse.

—Mark Twain
"Concerning the Jews," Harper's, September 1899

Semantics teaches us to watch our prejudices... Semantics is the propagandist's worst friend.

—Stuart Chase
Guides to Straight Thinking, 1956

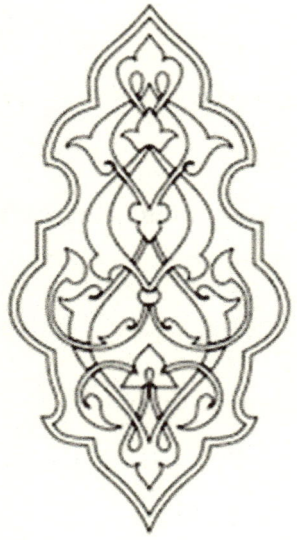

Quality versus Quantity

Quality versus Quantity | Eastern

The tree is known by its fruit.

—Christian scriptural proverb

For him who does everything in its proper place, one day is worth three.

—Chinese proverb

Good qualities, though hidden, become unveiled, and shine throughout the world. The flower of jasmine, although dried up, sends a sweet fragrance everywhere.

—Saskya Pandita

For every grass-blade its drop of dew.

—Chinese proverb

Quality versus Quantity | Western

Pauca Sed Matura
Few but Ripe

—Carl Friedrich Gauss

Good is not good, where better is expected.

—Thomas Fuller
The Church-History of Britain, 1655

Less is more.

—Robert Browning

Reason and Logic

Reason and Logic | Eastern

Do not believe what your teacher tells you merely out of respect.

—Buddha

Lower your voice and strengthen your argument.

—Lebanese proverb

Reason without a moral compass can go in any direction.

—Ghazali's philosophical thesis
Attributed

Virtue in its grandest aspect is neither more nor less than following reason.

—Lao Tzu

[Reason (al-'aql)] should govern, and not be governed; should control, and not be controlled; should lead, and not be led.

—Al-Razi
The Greatest Benefit to Mankind: A Medical History of Humanity

The "men of reason," [focus all their attention on the] form [while] men of vision [seek to transcend the] form.

—Ibn Arabi

Let reason, not impulse, be your guide.

—Kahlil Gibran
In Stanley Hendricks, Secrets of the Heart, 1968

We do most things relying only on our own sagacity we become selfinterested, turn our backs on reason, and things do not turn out well.

—Yamamoto Tsunetomo
Hagakure (In the Shadow of Leaves)

If a man possesses no knowledge of reasoning, he is incapable of expressing truth.

—Avicenna (Ibn Sina)
Avicenna on Theology, trans. Arberry

Al-Hashimi (cousin of Caliph al-Ma'mun) to a religious opponent:
Appoint some arbitrator who will impartially judge between us and lean only

towards the truth and be free from the empery of passion, and that arbitrator shall be reason.

—Al-Hashimi

Ahmad, I. A., "The Rise and Fall of Islamic Science: The Calendar as a Case Study," Faith and Reason: Convergence and Complementarity

When you discourse on learned subjects, speak after due reflection and say only that of which you can produce sufficient proof.

—Abu Hanifa

Imam Abu Hanifah, Life and Works

[I] am ready to accept whatever decision reason may give for me or against me.

—Al-Hashimi

Ahmad, I. A., "The Rise and Fall of Islamic Science: The Calendar as a Case Study," Faith and Reason: Convergence and Complementarity

Reason and logic | Western

If passion drives, let reason hold the reins.

—Benjamin Franklin
Poor Richard's Almanack, May 1749

In what does the movement of pure reason consist? To pose, oppose, and compose itself, to be formulated as thesis, antithesis and synthesis, or, better still, to affirm itself, to deny itself and to deny its negation.

—Karl Marx
The Poverty of Philosophy, 1847

I do not feel obliged to believe that the same God who has endowed us with senses, reason, and intellect has intended us to forgo their use and by some other means to give us knowledge which we can attain by them.

—Galileo
"Letter to the Grand Duchess Christina," 1615, Quoted in Aspects of Western Civilization:
Problems and Sources in History

Reasoning at every step he treads,
Man yet mistakes his way,
Whilst meaner things, whom instinct lead,
Are rarely known to stray.

—William Cowper
"The Doves," 1780

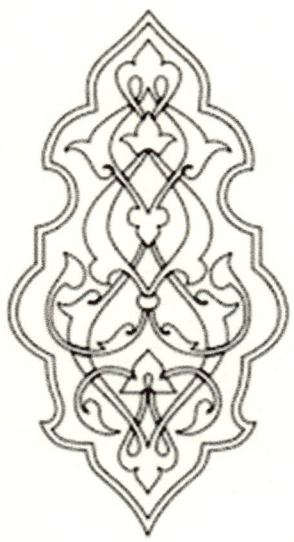

Revenge

Revenge | Eastern

Live well. It is the greatest revenge.

—The Talmud

Blood cannot be washed out with blood.

—Farci proverb

The way of revenge lies in simply forcing ones way into a place and being cut down.

—Yamamoto Tsunetomo

Revenge | Western

Perish the universe, so long as I have my revenge.

—Cryano De Bergerac

Revenge is the poor delight of little minds.

—Juvenal

Living well is the best revenge.

—George Herbert

A man that studieth revenge keeps his own wounds green.

—Francis Bacon

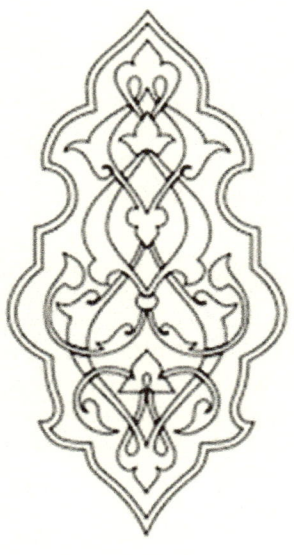

Risk

Risk | Eastern

Bullies are always to be found where there are cowards.

—Mahatma Gandhi

To see what is right and not do it is want of courage.

—Confucius

We must take all risks and go on doing the duties which by right are ours, though in the teeth of persecution.

—Rabindranath Tagore
1925 speech, The World's Great Speeches

Hold fast to truth in scorn of consequence.

—Islamic proverb

Krishnan: As long as I can stand, I will struggle.

—Mulk Raj Anand
The Bubble, 1984

My father taught me that you have to stand by your principles. He was president of the bar association and was preaching civil liberties and human rights during some of the most repressive years of the Nasser era. He was the focus of a lot of pressure and intimidation, but he stood by his principles. And I think that's a lesson I remember from him—that you stand up for what you believe in.

— Mohamed ElBaradei
"Breaking the Cycle," Cairo Times, October 23, 2003

Risk | Western

Carpe Diem
Seize the day

—Horace

Those who dare to fail miserably can achieve greatly.

—Robert F. Kennedy

The probability that we may fail in the struggle ought not to deter us from the support of a cause we believe to be just.

—Abraham Lincoln

Remember, you can't steal second if you don't take your foot off first.

—Mike Todd

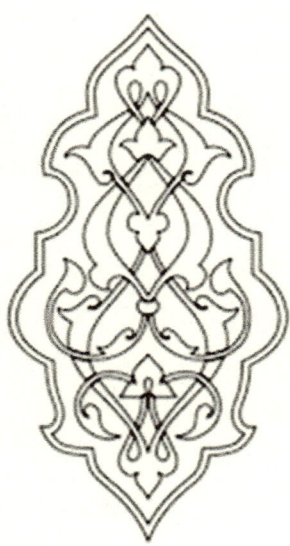

Silence

Silence | Eastern

The camps had taught him that people who kept silence bore something within themselves.

—Aleksandr Solzhenitsyn
Cancer Ward, trans. Rebecca Frank, 1968

Quiet water splits stone.

—Bengali proverb

Silence becomes cowardice when occasion demands speaking out the whole truth and acting accordingly.

—Mahatma Gandhi
In Harijan, April 1946

You know the sound of two hands clapping; tell me, what is the sound of one hand?

—Hakuin Ekaku

Silence is a friend who will never betray.

—Confucius
The Analects

Those who know do not talk
And talkers do not know.

—Lao-Tzu
The Way of Life, trans. R. B. Blakney, 1955

I never saw any lamp shining more brilliantly than the lamp of silence.

—Bayazid Bastami
Quoted in Tadhkiratul Awliya by Farid al-Din Attar

If Allah (God) wanted to punish a people, He would make them indulge in arguing and give up action. Many a times I have regretted speaking my son, but I have never regretted remaining silent.

—Hakeem Luqman

No one was angry enough to speak out.

—Inscription Found on Egyptian Pyramid
Quoted by Robert F. Kennedy

If speech is silver, silence is gold.

—Arabic proverb

Silent is the moonlight,
Silent the boughs of trees
Silent are the music makers of the valley,
And silent the green robed ones of the hills.
Creation is in a swoon
And asleep in the arms of the night.
The stillness has cast such a spell
That even the flow of the Neckar [river in Germany] seems still.
The caravan of the stars moves on
In silence, without bells.
Silent are hill and forest and river;
Nature seems lost in contemplation.
Thou too, o heart, be still!
Hold thy grief to thy bosom, and sleep.

—Iqbal
Mohammed Iqbal, Poet and Philosopher, trans. Mumtaz Hasan

Speak not, lie hidden, and conceal
the way you dream, the things you feel.
Deep in your spirit let them rise
akin to stars in crystal skies
that set before the night is blurred:
delight in them and speak no word.
How can a heart expression fi nd?
How should another know your mind?
Will he discern what quickens you?
A thought, once uttered, is untrue.
Dimmed is the fountainhead when stirred:
drink at the source and speak no word.
Live in your inner self alone
within your soul a world has grown,
the magic of veiled thoughts that might
be blinded by the outer light,
drowned in the noise of day, unheard...
take in their song and speak no word.

—Fyodor Ivanovich Tyutchev
trans. Vladimir Nabokov

Silence | Western

In the end, we will remember not the words of our enemies, but the silence of our friends.

—Martin Luther King Jr.

It is better to keep your mouth shut and appear stupid than to open it and remove all doubt.

—Mark Twain
Quoted in The Wit and Wisdom of Mark Twain

Silence is the mother of truth.

—Benjamin Disraeli
Tancred: Or, the New Crusade, 1847

We live in an age when silence is not only criminal but suicidal. If they take you in the morning they will be coming for us that night.

—James Baldwin
"Open Letter to My Sister, Miss Angela Davis," New York Review of Books, January 7, 1971

Silence is subversive—the womb of yet unborn cries of rebellion.

—Eric Hoffer
The Temper of Our Time, 1967

I get up very early in the morning. I enjoy the quietness, the stillness, the rawness in the winter and fall. It's a special time.

—Ted Kennedy
Esquire: The Meaning of Life, 2009

There comes a time when silence is dishonesty.

—Fanon
Toward the African Revolution: Political Essays

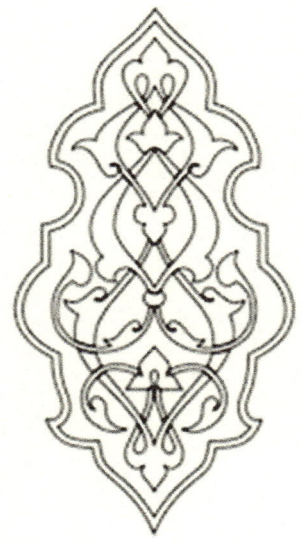

Science and Nature

Science and Nature | Eastern

What is beautiful by nature needs no adorning.

—Drishtana Sataka

If people do not revere [respect] the Law of Nature,
It will inexorably and adversely affect them.

—Lao Tzu

A flower falls even though we love it and a weed grows even though we do not love it.

—Zen proverb

When facing a single tree, if you look at a single one of its red leaves, you will not see all the others. When the eye is not set on one leaf, and you face the tree with nothing at all in mind, any number of leaves are visible to the eye without limit. But if a single leaf holds the eye, it will be as if the remaining leaves were not there.

— Takuan Soto

The sun will set without thy assistance.

—The Talmud

All that is by nature twain
Fears or suffers by the pain
Of separation.

—Dschami

Forget not that the earth delights to feel your bare feet and the winds long to play with your hair.

—Kahlil Gibran

Nature does not hurry, yet everything is accomplished.

—Lao Tzu

Science and Nature | Western

Nature to be commanded must be obeyed.

—Francis Bacon

The earth is a living organism, and I'll stick by it.

—James Lovelock
A History of Knowledge: Past, Present, and Future, Charles Van Doren

Nature is very consonant and comfortable with herself.

— Isaac Newton

There is no unemployed force in nature. All decomposition is recomposition.

—Ralph Waldo Emerson

There are many wonderful things in nature, but the most wonderful of all is man.

—Sophocles

Nature, red in tooth and claw.

—Lord Alfred Tennyson

It is wrong to think that the task of physics is to find out how nature is. Physics concerns what we can say about nature.

—Niels Bohr

In all things of nature there is something of the marvelous.

—Aristotle

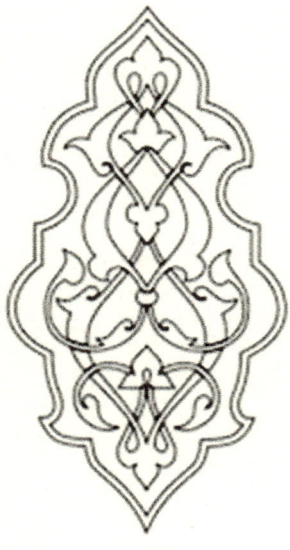

Time

Time | Eastern

There is no hand to catch time.

—Bengali proverb

The Bird of Time has but a little way
To flutter—and Lo! the Bird is on the Wing

—Omar Khayyam
Quoted in The Rubaiyat of Omar Khayyam, trans. Fitzgerald

Timing in strategy cannot be mastered without a great deal of practice.
—Miyamoto Musashi
Go Rin No Sho (The Book of Five Rings), 1645

Today is a bubble
Beautiful and multi-coloured
Floating down the river of Time.

—Gobala Reddy
Mulk Raj Anand: The Novel of Commitment, 2000

Time never gets tired of running.

—Amad

Time: a great engraver, or eraser.

—Yahia Lababidi
Signposts to Elsewhere, 2008

Time | Western

O, call back yesterday, bid time return!

—Shakespeare

Time has no divisions to mark its passage; there is never a thunderstorm to announce the beginning of a new year. It is only we mortals who ring bells and fire off pistols.

—Thomas Mann
The Magic Mountain (Knopf)

This thing all things devours:
Birds, beasts, trees, flowers;
Gnaws iron, bites steel,
Grinds hard stones to meal;
Slays king, ruins town,
And beats high mountain down.

—J. R. R. Tolkien
The Hobbit. The answer is "Time"

The surest poison is time.

—Ralph Waldo Emerson

And what if you were told: One more hour?

—Elias Canetti

The only reason time is so that everything does not happen at once.
—Albert Einstein

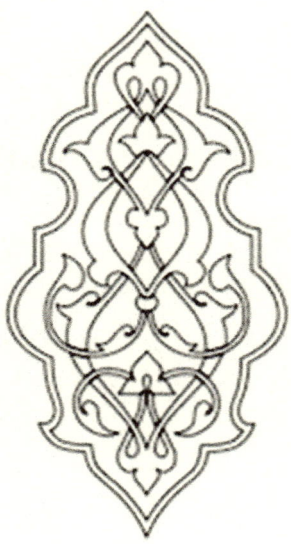

Universe

Universe | Eastern

Astrology is a disease, not a science... It is a tree under the shadow of which all sorts of superstitions thrive... Only fools and charlatans lend value to it.

—Moses Maimon (Maimonides)
Letter to Marseilles, 1195, "Responsa," ii, 25b

We must, therefore, apply ourselves to a new investigation concerning that genuine astronomy whose foundations are principles of physics.

—Averroes

Some of our friends have become fond of hashish—it's the devil's fantasy... Why don't our friends taste the pure and endless universe of ours?

—Shams of Tabriz

The universe and I exist together, and all things and I are one.

—Chuang Tzu

This universe is a drop from the ocean of His beauty,
unable from its fullness to find place in the parent bosom.

—Rumi

Every moment of your life is infinitely creative and the universe is endlessly bountiful.

—Mahatma Gandhi

Universe | Western

To understand the Universe, you must understand the language in which it's written the language of mathematics.

—Galileo

The Universe is represented in an atom. In a moment in time.

—Ralph Waldo Emerson

The universe, as far as we can observe it, is a wonderful and immense engine; its extent, its order, its beauty its cruelty, make it alike impressive... Great is this organism of mud and fire, terrible this vast, painful, glorious experiment.

—George Santayana
The Life of Reason: Reason in Religion, 1905

From the intrinsic evidence of the his creation, the Great Architect of the Universe now begins to appear as a pure mathematician.

—James Jeans

All things are connected with all things throughout the universe, from the insect to the archangel; from the sand-grain to the mountain and the globe; from the dew-drop to the ocean; from the rain-drop to the rainbow; from the pebble on the shore to "the sun that blazes in the firmament; from the zephyr that sings among the flowers of the field to the ocean that pours its wild bass in the great anthem of nature." Not only are all things connected with all things, but there is a concatenation of events, so that the character and effects of no one event can terminate in itself.

—John Lanahan
Reported in Josiah Hotchkiss Gilbert, Dictionary of Burning Words of Brilliant Writers,
1895

Secrets

Secrets | Eastern

Unless silence makes you an accomplice, never betray a man's secret.

—Ben Sira

When you give, let not your left hand know what your right hand does.

—Christian proverb

Whoever wants to hear my words must come into my inner universe, but there is a doorkeeper.

—Shams of Tabriz
Rumi's Sun: The Teachings of Shams of Tabriz, 2008

If you reveal your secrets to the wind you should not blame the wind for revealing them to the trees.

—Kahlil Gibran
Sand and Foam

He who guards his secrets retains control in his own hands.

—Ali

Don't be worried that the world gives not out its secret,
For what the rose cannot say, the complaining bird can.

—Iqbal
Quoted in Gabriel's Wing, by Annemarie Schimmel

One who keeps his secrets controls his affairs.

—Umar

Secrets | Western

In nature's infinite book of secrecy
A little I can read.

—Shakespeare

If you would keep your Secret from an enemy,
tell it not to a friend.

—Benjamin Franklin
Poor Richard's Almanack, July 1735

And whatsoever else shall hap tonight,
Give it an understanding, but no tongue.

—Shakespeare
Hamlet

There are no secrets to success. It is the result of preparation, hard work, and learning from failure.

—Colin Powell

The secret of getting ahead is getting started. The secret of getting started is breaking your complex overwhelming tasks into small manageable tasks, and then starting on the first one.

—Mark Twain

Solitude

Solitude | Eastern

Now the New Year reviving old Desires,
The thoughtful Soul to Solitude retires.

—Omar Khayyam
Quoted in The Rubaiyat of Omar Khayyam, trans. Fitzgerald

The earth is a beehive; we all enter by the same door but live in different cells.
—African proverb

Solitude | Western

I lived in solitude in the country and noticed how the monotony of a quiet life stimulates the creative mind.

—Albert Einstein
Speech, Albert Hall, London, October 1933

We're all of us sentenced to solitary confinement inside our own skins, for life!
—Tennessee Williams
Orpheus Descending, 2.1, 1957

Spiritual: Meditation and Prayer

Spiritual: Meditation and Prayer | Eastern

Be still and know.

—Chinese proverb

Prayer is man's attempt to speak to God. Meditation is man's attempt to listen to God.

—Sufi proverb

Both in fighting and in everyday life you should be determined though calm.

—Miyamoto Musashi
Go Rin No Sho (The Book of Five Rings), 1645

Meditation is the action of silence.

—Krishnamurti
Meditations

The Heart's cry to God is the sincerest prayer.

—Ancient Jewish proverb

The act of goodness surpasses a thousand prayers.

—Sa'di
Quoted in The Maxims of Sa'di

Allah (God) loves the [faithful] scholar more than a thousand worshipers.

—Islamic proverb

Spiritual: Meditation and Prayer | Western

The family that prays together stays together.

—Al Scalpone

Pray to God only for things which you cannot obtain from man.

—Pope Sixtus I

Pray devoutly and hammer stoutly.

—English language proverb

To meditate is to observe simultaneously the formation of thought and breath, and then let it go, without complicating it, without formalizing it, without identifying it, without rejecting it, letting it follow its own way.

—Allen Ginsberg
Jean-Jacques Lebel interview, Le Monde, June 1, 1979

We call prayer… that speech of man to God which, whatever else is asked, ultimately asks for the manifestation of the divine presence.

—Martin Buber
Eclipse of God: Studies in the Relation between Religion and Philosophy,
trans. Maurice S. Friedman, 1952

Wisdom is intuitive knowledge of the mind of love and clarity that lies beneath one's ego-driven anxieties and aggressions. Meditation is going into the mind to see this for yourself—over and over again, until it becomes the mind you live in.

—Gary Snyder
"Buddhism and the Coming Revolution," Earth House Hold:
Technical Notes & Queries to Fellow Dharma Revolutionaries

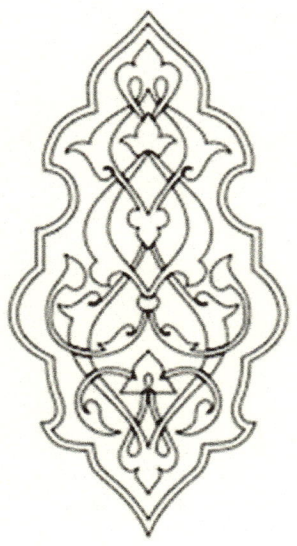

Success

Success | Eastern

Success for the most part attends those who act boldly, not those who weigh everything, and are [slow] to venture.

—Xerxes
Quoted by Herodotus, The Persian Wars, 7.50, trans. George Rawlinson, 1942

Power is given only to those who dare to lower themselves and pick it up.

—Fyodor Dostoevsky

For what shall it profit a man, if he shall gain the whole world, and lose his own soul?

—Christian proverb

With faith, discipline and selfless devotion to duty, there is nothing worthwhile that you cannot achieve.

—Jinnah
Address to the officers, February 21, 1948

If you wish to be out front,
Then act as if you were behind.

—Lao-Tzu
The Way of Life, 66, trans. R. B. Blakney, 1955

The will to win, the desire to succeed, the urge to reach your full potential... these are the keys that will unlock the door to personal excellence.

—Confucius

Success | Western

I have not failed. I've just found 10,000 ways that won't work.

—Thomas Edison

I came, I saw, I conquered.

—Julius Caesar

Try not to become a man of success but rather to become a man of value.

—Albert Einstein

That's one small step for a man, one great leap for mankind.

—Neil Armstrong

I don't know the key to success, but the key to failure is trying to please everybody.

—Bill Cosby

Eighty percent of success is showing up.

—Woody Allen

In Thomas J. Peters and Robert H. Walterman Jr., In Search of Excellence:
Lessons from
America's Best-Run Companies, 1982

True happiness is not attained through self-gratification, but through fidelity to a worthy purpose.

—Helen Keller

One overmuch elated with success
A change of fortune plunges in distress.

—Horace
Casper J. Kraemer Jr., The Complete Works of Horace, 1936

Find a need and fill it.

—Henry Kaiser

Tis a lesson you should heed,
Try, try again.
If at first you don't succeed,
Try, try again.

—William Edward Hickson

Try and Try Again

Nothing comes easy. Nothing is given to you. Whatever you do, you've got to work for it and earn it.

—Jack Charlton
From his interview with Martyn Lewis, in his book, Reflections on Success, 1997

The man who wins may have been counted out several times, but he didn't hear the referee.

—H. E. Jansen

W. Dennis Thomas: Would you explain the secret of your success as head of Merrill Lynch?
Regan: That's not a big conversation. It's one word—anticipation.

—Donald T. Regan

In Gerald M. Boyd, "General Contractor' of the White House Staff," New York Times,
March 4, 1986

Whoever desires constant success must change his conduct with the times.

—Machiavelli

The Discourses, 1517, trans. Christian E. Detmold, 1940

What is success?
To laugh often and much;
To win the respect of intelligent people
And the affection of children;
To earn the appreciation of honest critics
And endure the betrayal of false friends;
To appreciate beauty;
To find the best in others;
To leave the world a bit better, whether by
A healthy child, a garden patch
Or a redeemed social condition;
To know even one life has breathed
Easier because you have lived;
This is to have succeeded.

—Ralph Waldo Emerson

Failure is an orphan, success has many fathers.

—Anonymous

Success breeds success.

—Anonymous

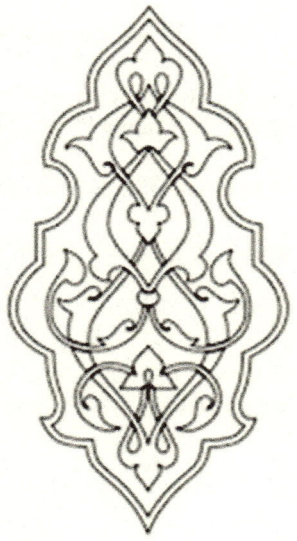

Suffering and Adversity

Suffering and Adversity | Eastern

Suffering is a gift. In it is hidden mercy.

—Rumi

Pearls unpolished shine not.

—Japanese proverb

At the extremity of hardship comes relief, and at the tightening of the chains of tribulation comes ease.

—Ali
Nahj al-Balagha (Peak of Eloquence)

Your tireless and heroic sacrifices have made it possible for me to be here today. I therefore place the remaining years of my life in your hands.

—Nelson Mandala
Speech on the day of his release, Cape Town, February 11, 1990

All your suffering comes from desiring things that cannot be had. Stop desiring and you won't suffer.

—Rumi
Attributed

A gem is not polished without rubbing, nor is a man
perfected without trials.

—Chinese proverb

The free feel sorrow
No more than a moment;
In our house of lamentation
We light the candle from the lightening.

—Mirza Ghalib
Quoted in Natalia Prigarina, Mirza Ghalib: A Creative Biography

I never lamented about the vicissitudes of time or complained of the turns of fortune except on the occasion when I was barefooted and unable to procure slippers. But when I entered the great mosque of Kufah with a sore heart and beheld a man without feet I offered thanks to the bounty of God, consoled myself for my want of shoes and recited:
"A roast fowl is to the sight of a satiated man

Less valuable than a blade of fresh grass on the table
And to him who has no means nor power
A burnt turnip is a roasted fowl."

—Sa'di
Gulistan

Suffering and Adversity | Western

Oh, how bitter a thing is to look through another man's eye.

—Shakespeare

He knows not his own strength that hath not met adversity.

Francis Bacon

Adversity introduces a man to himself.

—Anonymous

He whom prosperity humbles, and adversity strengthens, is the true hero.

—Josh Billings
Josh Billing's Encyclopedia and Proverbial Philosophy of Wit and Humor, 1874

There is no education like adversity.

—Benjamin Disraeli

Search for the seed of good in every adversity.

—Og Mandino

Time eases all things.

—Sophocles
Oedipus Rex

Misery acquaints a man with strange bedfellows.

—Shakespeare
The Tempest

Inside a ring or out, ain't nothing wrong with going down. It's saying down that's wrong.

—Muhammad Ali (Cassius Clay)

Compare your grief with those of other men and they will seem less so.

—Spanish proverb

There is no such thing as suffering without cause or blame.

—Edward Said

Expect trouble as an inevitable part of life, and when it comes, hold your head high, look it squarely in the eye and say, "I will be bigger than you. You cannot defeat me."

—Ann Landers

I've learned that people will forget what you said, people will forget what you did, but people will never forget how you made them feel.

—Maya Angelou

It is said an Eastern monarch once charged his wise men to invent him a sentence, to be ever in view, and which should be true and appropriate in all times and situations. They presented him the words: "And this, too, shall pass away." How much it expresses! How chastening in the hour of pride! How consoling in the depths of affliction!

—Abraham Lincoln
In his address "Before the Wisconsin State Agricultural Society, Milwaukee, Wisconsin,"
September 30, 1859

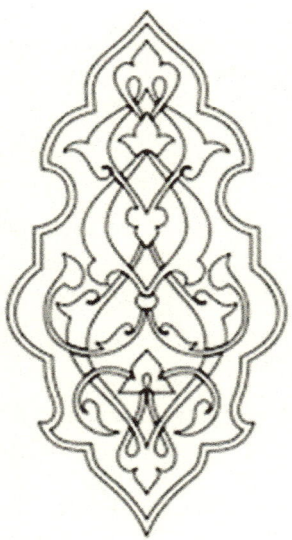

Truth

Truth | Eastern

The object of the superior man is truth.

—Confucius
The Analects

The most excellent struggle is to speak up for truth in the face of a tyrannical authority.

—Muhammad
Ahmad ibn Hanbal, 18074

After a hundred million subtleties, sophisms, and lies, the smallest truth remains precisely what it was before.

—Chinese proverb

Whoever clashes with truth would be knocked down by it.

—Ali
Nahj al-Balagha (Peak of Eloquence)

Bodies are cleansed by water; the mind by truth.

— South Asian proverb
Quoted in Al-Ghazali, trans. McCarthy

An exaggeration is a truth that has lost its temper.

—Kahlil Gibran

Truth is the greatest gift and the height of duty.

—Narada Smriti

He says, "O Sun! don't radiate any more divine light, so that the hearts of the bats may not be hurt."
But this is the business of the sun; of course it will radiate light.
Would it ever stop shining so that the eyes of the bats might not be hurt? He said, "The sun isn't troubled by bats or those with weak eyes. It just keeps radiating light."
—Shams of Tabriz
Rumi's Sun: The Teachings of Shams of Tabriz, 2008

You cannot live without truth because the whole universe lives by the truth.
—Amr Khaled
"In Thy Name, We live," Episode 17, Al-Haqq (The Truth)

Hence to fight and conquer in all our battles is not supreme excellence; supreme excellence consists in breaking the enemy's resistance without fighting.

—Sun Tzu

Always speak the truth, so that you get the right advice.

—Abu Bakr

Truth prevails, falsehood vanishes.

—Qur'an 17:81

Truth | Western

When in doubt, tell the truth.

—Mark Twain

All truths wait in all things,
They neither hasten their own delivery nor resist it.

—Walt Whitman

Plato is dear to me, but dearer still is truth.

—Aristotle

Truth is on the march; nothing now can stop it.

—Emile Zola
J'accuse...!

Truth in the human mind consists in the mind's conformity to reality to that which is.

—St. Thomas Aquinas

The opposite of a correct statement is a false statement. But the opposite of a profound truth may well be another profound truth.

—Niels Bohr
Heisenberg

When a thing is funny, search it for a hidden truth.

—George Bernard Shaw

Tell the truth and shame the devil.

—Francois Rabelais

When you have eliminated the impossible, whatever remains, however improbable, must be the truth.

—Sir Arthur Conan Doyle

Just as light reveals both itself and the darkness, so truth is the standard of itself and of the thoughts.

—Spinoza

To a new truth there is nothing more harmful than old error.

—Goethe

Christians should never think they honor the greater truth they find in Christ by ignoring truths found elsewhere.

—Reverend William Sloan Coffin

The truth is rarely pure, and never simple.

—Oscar Wilde

Plato says, "a false proposition, "that is, a false statement, "is one which asserts the nonexistence of things which are or the existence of things which are not." "To say of what is that it is or of what is not that it is not, is to speak the truth or to think truly just as it is false to say of what is that it is not or of what is not that it is."

—Aristotle

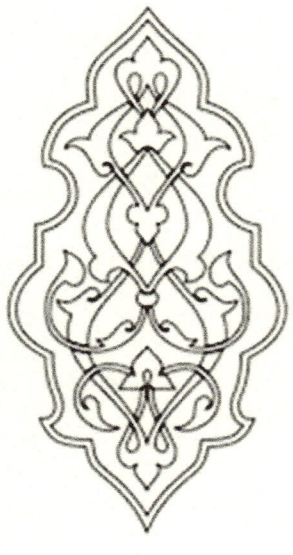

Vanity

Vanity | Eastern

O vanity! You are the lever by means of which Archimedes wished to lift the earth!

—Mikhail Yuryevich Lermontov
A Hero of Our Time, 1839

How does one whose origin is semen and whose end is a carcass dare be vain?

—Arab couplet

Vanity | Western

Nothing so soothes our vanity as a display of greater vanity in others; it makes us vain, in fact, of our modesty.

—Louis Kronenberger
"Aphorisms," Vogue, March 1, 1964

Vain-Glory Flowereth, but beareth no Fruit.

—Benjamin Franklin
Poor Richard's Almanack, 1756

On some positions, Cowardice asks the question, "Is it safe?"
Expediency asks the question, "Is it politic?" And Vanity comes along and asks the question, "Is it popular?" But Conscience asks the question "Is it right?"

—Martin Luther King Jr.
"Remaining Awake Through a Great Revolution," March 31, 1968

Beauty's sister is vanity, and its daughter lust.

—Anonymous

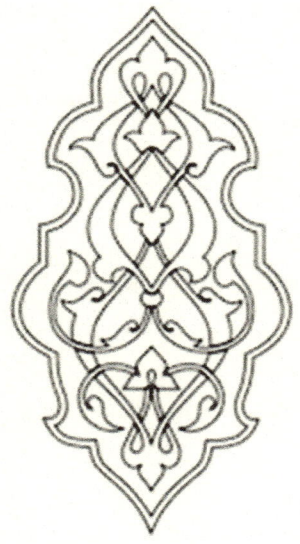

War and Conflict

War and conflict | Eastern

The clever hawk hides its claws.

—Japanese proverb

Fire springs from the rubbing of sticks, and warfare from the wagging of tongues.

—Caliph Marwan
The new encyclopedia of Islam, by Cyril Glassé, Huston Smith

War is a respectable term for goondaism [hooliganism] practiced on a mass or national scale.

—Mahatma Gandhi
Quoted in Harijan, September 15, 1946

My sword is sharp and terrible. It is the mightiest of things when the pot of war boils fiercely.

—Khalid ibn Walid

Force does not heal old wounds; it opens new ones.

—Mohamed ElBaradei
Nobel lecture, 2005

You will kill ten of our men, and we will kill one of yours, and in the end it will be you who tire of it.

—Ho Chi Minh

It is said the warrior's is the twofold Way of pen and sword, and he should have a taste for both Ways.

—Miyamoto Musashi

Go Rin No Sho (The Book of Five Rings), 1645

To lead an uninstructed people to war, is to throw them away.

—Confucius
The Analects

Strategy is the craft of the warrior.

—Miyamoto Musashi
Go Rin No Sho (The Book of Five Rings), 1645

Honour the enemy's envoy.

—Abu Bakr
In Ghulam Sarwar, Islam Beliefs and Teachings

In modern war there is no such thing as victor and vanquished.... [T] here is only a loser, and that loser is mankind.

—U Thant
Address, Economic Club, New York, 1963

Abu Bakr (First Caliph), in the form of ten rules for the army: "Stop, O people, that I may give you ten rules for your guidance in the battlefield. Do not commit treachery or deviate from the right path. You must not mutilate dead bodies. Neither kill a child, nor a woman, nor an aged man. Bring no harm to the trees, nor burn them with fire, especially those which are fruitful. Slay not any of the enemy's flock, save for your food. You are likely to pass by people who have devoted their lives to monastic services; leave them alone."

—Abu Bakr
Aboul-Enein, H. Yousuf, and Zuhur, Sherifa, Islamic Rulings on Warfare, Strategic Studies Institute, US Army War College

The beginning of war starts with words.

—Arabic proverb

Very often the hero of one is a foe of the other.

—Abul Kalam Azad
Quoted in Eight Lives: A Study of the Hindu-Muslim Encounter

And here I am, dying in my bed, like cattle die. May the eyes of cowards never sleep.

—Khalid ibn Walid
Last words by the General

Governments need armies to protect them from their enslaved and oppressed subjects.

—Leo Tolstoy

Strength does not come from physical capacity. It comes from an indomitable will.

—Mahatma Gandhi
Quoted in Young India, August 11, 1920

The effect of the oppression on us has passed away, but it will remain on the oppressor (forever).

—Persian Couplet

Brute force only breaks; it does not mend and fix.

—Akbar the Great
Attributed

War and Conflict | Western

To hold a pen is to be at war.

—Voltaire
Letter to Jeanne-Grâce Bosc du Bouchet, comtesse d'Argental

There is only one decisive victory: the last.

—Karl Von Clausewitz

The worst barbarity of war is that it forces men collectively to commit acts against which individually they would revolt with their whole being.

—Ellen Key
War, Peace, and the Future, 1916

A nation that continues year after year to spend more money on military defense than on programs of social uplift is approaching spiritual death.

—Martin Luther King Jr.
"Declaration of Independence from the War in Vietnam," April 4, 1967

When the rich make war it's the poor that die.

—Jean-Paul Sartre

War. . . is an act of violence intended to compel our opponent to fulfill our will.

—Carl Von Clausewitz
On War, 1832, trans. J. J. Graham, 1873

Mankind has grown great in eternal struggles, and only in eternal peace does it perish.

—Adolph Hitler
Mein Kamph, 1924, trans. Ralph Manheim, 1943

No more war, war never again! Peace, it is peace which must guide the destinies of peoples and of all mankind.

—Pope Paul VI
United Nations address, New York City, October 4, 1965

In a crisis, both data and policy outpace analysis.

—Richard Betts
"Analysis War and Decision: Why Intelligence Failures Are Inevitable," World Politics 31, no. 1, October 1978

A terrorist is someone who has a bomb but can't afford an air force.

—William Blum

In the councils of government, we must guard against the acquisition of unwarranted influence, whether sought or unsought, by the military-industrial complex.

—Dwight d. Eisenhower
Farewell address, January 17, 1961

Every war when it comes, or before it comes, is represented not as a war but as an act of self-defense against a homicidal maniac.

—George Orwell

During wartime military organizations are "in business."

—Stephen Peter Rosen
Winning the Next War: Innovation and the Modern Military, 1991

Mark this well, you proud men of action! You are, after all, nothing but unconscious instruments of the men of thought.

—Georg Friedrich Hegel

War is the greatest test of a bureaucratic organization.

—James Q. Wilson
Bureaucracy: What Government Agencies Do and Why They Do It

[Strategy] is the art of making war upon the map.

—Baron de Jomini
The Art of War

A great part of the information obtained in war is contradictory, a still greater part is false, and by far the greatest part is of a doubtful character.

—Carl Von Clausewitz
Quoted in On War, 1985

[T]he taproot of suicide terrorism is nationalism [not religion]… [It is] an extreme strategy for national liberation.

—Robert Pape
Dying to Win: The Strategic Logic of Suicide Terrorism, 2005

I ain't got no quarrel with the Vietcong…
No Vietcong ever called me n—.

—Muhammad Ali (Cassius Clay)

Tactics is the theory of the use of military forces in combat. Strategy is the theory of the use of combat for the object of War.

—Carl Von Clausewitz
Quoted in On War, 1985

Voice or no voice, the people can always be brought to the bidding of the leaders. That is easy. All you have to do is to tell them they are being attacked, and denounce the pacifists for lack of patriotism and exposing the country to danger.

—Hermann Goering

It's hard to stop a war if you don't talk with those who are involved in it.

—George Mitchell

Genuine tragedies in the world are not conflicts between right and wrong. They are conflicts between two rights.

—Georg Friedrich Hegel

War is not merely a political act, but also a real political instrument, a continuation of political commerce, a carrying out of the same by other means.

—Karl Von Clausewitz
On War, 1832, trans. J. J. Graham, 1873

I hold that a little rebellion, now and then, is a good thing.

—Thomas Jefferson
A Letter from Thomas Jefferson to James Madison, 1787

The triumph of persuasion over force is the sign of a civilized society.

—Mark Skousen

I and mind do not convince by arguments, similes, rhymes,
We convince by our presence.

—Walt Whitman
"Song of the Open Road," Leaves of Grass, 1856

Persuasion deals in the coin of self-interest.

—Richard E. Neustadt

If you would win a man to your cause, first convince him that you are his sincere friend.

—Abraham Lincoln
Address before the Washington Temperance Society, Springfield (Illinois), February 22, 1842

He who wants to persuade should put his trust not in the right argument, but in the right word. The power of sound has always been greater than the power of sense... Give me the right word and the right accent, and I will move the world.

—Joseph Conrad
"A Familiar Preface," A Personal Record, 1923
Presidential Power: The Politics of Leadership, 1960

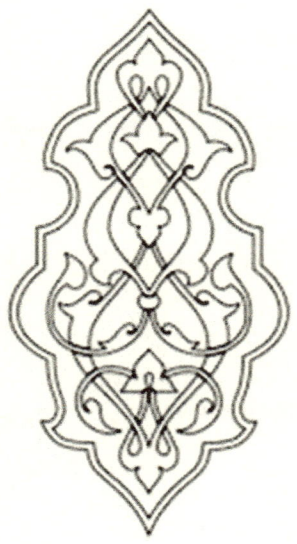

Strong and Weak

Strong and Weak | Eastern

The oppressed and the oppressor alike are robbed of their humanity.

—Nelson Mandela
Long Walk to Freedom

I am not interested in picking up crumbs of compassion thrown from the table of someone who considers himself my master. I want the full menu of rights.

—Desmond M. Tutu
Today, NBC TV, January 9, 1985

He kills the victim and walks in his funeral.

—Egyptian proverb

Strength does not come from physical capacity. It comes from an indomitable will.

—Mahatma Gandhi
Quoted in Young India, August 11, 1920

The effect of the oppression on us has passed away, but it will remain on the oppressor (forever).

—Persian Couplet

China is an attractive piece of meat coveted by all... but very tough, and for years no one has been able to bite into it.

—Zhou Enlai
"To Chinese Communist Party Congress," New York Times, September 1, 1973

If you are neutral in situations of injustice, you have chosen the side of the oppressor.

—Desmond M. Tutu
As quoted in Ending Poverty As We Know It: Guaranteeing a Right to a Job at a
Living Wage,
by William P. Quigley

We must abandon the unworkable notion that it is morally reprehensible for some countries to pursue weapons of mass destruction yet morally acceptable for others to rely on them for security—and indeed to continue to refi ne their capacities and postulate plans for their use.

—Mohamed ElBaradei
"Saving Ourselves From Self-Destruction," New York Times, February 12, 2004

Today is victory over yourself of yesterday; tomorrow is your victory over lesser men.

—Miyamoto Musashi
Go Rin No Sho (The Book of Five Rings), 1645

It is possible for a single individual to defy the whole might of an unjust empire to save his honor, his religion, his soul, and lay the foundations for that empire's fall or its regeneration.

—Mahatma Gandhi

As soon as men live entirely in accord with the law of love natural to their hearts... not only will hundreds be unable to enslave millions, but not even millions will be able to enslave a single individual.

—Leo Tolstoy
A Letter to a Hindu

Strong and Weak | Western

Power always thinks it has a great soul and vast views beyond the comprehension of the weak.

—John Adams

It is human nature to hate the person whom you have hurt.

—Publius Cornelius Tacitus

Colonialism forces the colonized to constantly ask the question, "Who am I in reality?"

—Franz Fanon
Wretched of the Earth

He that makes himself a sheep shall be eaten [by] the wolf.

—John Clarke
Proverbs: English and Latin

The concessions of the weak, are the concessions of fear.

—Edmund Burke
"Conciliation with America," House of Commons speech, March 22, 1775

At its most powerful, colonialism is a process of radical dispossession. A colonized people is without a specific history and even, as in Ireland and other cases, without a specific language.

—Seamus Deane

Wisdom

Wisdom | Eastern

Collect as precious pearls the words of those who are as an ocean of knowledge and virtue.

—Turkish proverb

In every head is some wisdom.

—Arabic proverb

Wisdom is not acquired save as the result of investigation.

—Sankara Acharya
Quoted in Britannica

The hearts become tired as the bodies become tired. You should therefore search for beautiful sayings for them (to enjoy by way of refreshment).

—Ali
Nahj al-Balagha (Peak of Eloquence)

Wisdom | Western

The doors of wisdom are never shut.

—Benjamin Franklin

The wisdom of the wise and the experience of the ages are perpetuated by quotations.

—Benjamin Disraeli

Wisdom is a curse when wisdom does nothing for the man who has it.

—Sophocles
Oedipus Rex

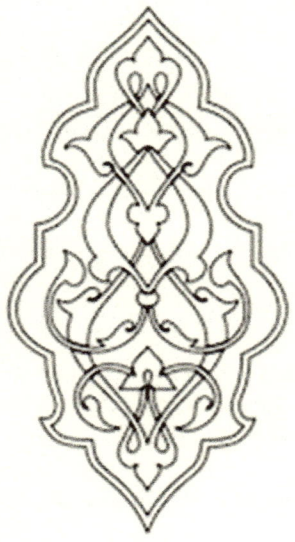

Words/Speech

Words/Speech | Eastern

The tongue is but three inches long, yet can kill a man six feet tall.

—Japanese proverb

A society with only one voice is by no means a stable society.

—Statement by 500 Beijing University Faculty on Peaceful Pro-
Democracy Demonstrations in China
The World's Great Speeches

The tongue is a beast; if it is let loose, it devours.

—Ali
Nahj al-Balagha (Peak of Eloquence)

Each human being is a "word" spoken by God.

—Shams of Tabriz
Rumi's Sun: The Teachings of Shams of Tabriz, 2008

The superior man is modest in his speech, exceeds in his actions.

—Confucius
The Analects

Be careful of your speech; a flaw in jade may be
ground away, but a fl aw in speech is hopeless.

—Chinese proverb

Right to freedom of speech must not be imperilled.

—Ali
Quoted in Justice and Democracvy by Ronald Bontekoe

What flowers are to gardens, spices to food, gems to garment, and stars to
heaven, such are proverbs interwoven in speech.

—Hebrew proverb
Quoted in Pebbles, Pearls and Gems of the Orient, no. 477, 1882

Be careful of your speech; a flaw in jade may be ground away, but a flaw in
speech is hopeless.

—Chinese proverb

'eza kan el-kalam min faDah fa el-sukoot min dahab
If speech is silver, silence is gold.

—Arabic proverb

A superior man is modest in his speech, but exceeds in his actions.
—Confucius
The Analects

Staying quiet at the proper time is a characteristic of manhood, just as speaking when it is proper to speak is from the most honorable of matters.
—Abul Qaasim al-Qushayri
Risaalah

In debating be courageous and steadfast; if you have the slightest fear in your heart you will not be able to keep your thoughts collected and your tongue will stammer. Never get involved in discussion with people who do not know the rules of debate or who become unpleasant.

—Abu Hanifa
Imam Abu Hanifah, Life and Works

Word/Speech | Western

Carve every word before you let it fall.

—Oliver Wendell Holmes

What orators lack in depth they make up to you in length.

—Charles de Montesquieu

Speak, that I may see thee.

—Ben Johnson *Adepts in the speaking trade*

Keep a cough by them ready made.

—Charles Churchill

Abuse of words has been the great instrument of sophistry and chicanery of party, faction, and division of society.

—John Adams

I do not much dislike the matter, but the manner of his speech.

—Shakespeare

If the freedom of speech is taken away then dumb and silent we may be led, like sheep to the slaughter.

—George Washington

What comes from the tongue reaches the mind, what comes from the heart reaches the heart.

—Anonymous

The most valuable of all talents is that of never using two words when one will do.

—Thomas Jefferson

Broadly speaking, the short words are the best, and the old words best of all.

—Winston Churchill
"Riches of English Language," speech, 1947, Winston Churchill:
His Complete Speeches 1897-1963, vol. 7, ed. Robert R. James, 1974

Words are like leaves; and where they most abound,
Much fruit of sense beneath is rarely found.

—Alexander Pope

As with all good things...

The End

Made in the USA
Las Vegas, NV
13 August 2021